Turns in the Road

Turns in the Road
Companions on
the Journey

Editorial Committee
Larry Egan, Tom Fenton, Darryl Hunt, George Laudadio,
Frank Maurovich, Bill Murphy, Al Stumph

2011

Photographs that appear in this book were selected and pro-
cessed for publication by Ray Voith ('70) from the archive of
Maryknoll-related photographs that he created and maintains:
www.voith-usa.com/SemPix/indexToSempix.html. We acknowl-
edge and thank Ray for his efforts. Photo credits: Jack Clancey,
121; FAO, 158; Tom Fenton, 126; Don Goulet, 18, 184, 196;
Maryknoll at Work in the World, 42, 62, 114; Maryknoll Mission
Center (Cochabamba), 47; Maryknoll Society Archives, 10; Fr.
Dennis Moorman, M.M., 140; John T. Moran, 32, 155; Bill
Murphy, 162; Stan Sztaba, 143, 167; Fr. Joe Towle, M.M., 149.
Apologies for any photographs we failed to credit properly. —
The Editors

ISBN-13: 978-1463758684
ISBN-10: 1463758685

Contents

Para los Pobres, by Bob Maxwell ('56) 11

Reflections on the Relationship of the Maryknoll Society
  with Resigned Maryknollers, by Jerry Murphy ('58) 13

Five More Years, by James C. O'Connor ('63) 16

Maryknoll's Influence in My Life, by Joe Fahey ('67) 20

Swings and Roundabouts, by Robert Connolly ('79) 25

Marrying a Former Priest, by Florence McGuire,
  wife of P. Thomas McGuire ('67) 31

Turns in the Road: Companions on the Journey,
  by John Sullivan, M.M. ('60) 34

Always Connected, by Hank Gromada ('67) 43

Maryknoll Reflections, by Jim MacDonald ('68) 45

Ugali, by Bill Murphy ('71) 49

Faith of a Mustard Seed, by Frank Luciani ('74) 51

Maryknoll and Me: Part of the Story, by Tom Quigley ('57) 53

How I Came to Maryknoll, Learned from Maryknoll,
  Left Maryknoll, And What Happened Afterwards,
  by Nick Petraglia ('60) 57

Some Grateful Thoughts, by Andy Eichmann ('68) 59

A Maryknoll Story, by Bill Allen ('57) 61

Maryknoll's Micaiah, by Jim Collignon ('53) 64

Invitations and Camaraderie, by Jack Clancey ('68) 69

Maryknoll's Impact: The First 100 Years, by Donald Howard ('69) . . 73

What Being a Missionary Meant to Me, or My Life
  in the Philippines, by Robert Nugent ('66) 75

A Priest Forever, by Joe Bukovchik ('66) 82

What Does Maryknoll Mean to Me? by Steve Cuthbertson ('71) . . . 88

Global Vision, by Dan Driscoll-Shaw ('66) 91

The Joy of the Road, by John K. Halbert, M.M. ('59) 93

Acceptance of Challenging Life Events, by LeRoy Spaniol ('66) . . . 95

A Tremendous Liberation, by John T. Moran ('70) 99

This Is Thy Aim, Thy Sacred Call, by Art Melville ('61) 103

The Continuity of Life, A Little Patch of Green, by Bill Mersch ('71) . 105

Men for Others, by Bob McGuire ('71) 108

Entrance into a New World, by Vic Hummert ('67) 118

A Continuing Quest, by Ron DuBois ('63) 123

My Life and the Influence of Maryknoll Training on It,
  by Bob O'Neil ('68) 124

Three Ideas: A Tongue-in-Cheek Reflection, by Thomas
  Whaling ('61) 128

Uncle Bill, by Christopher Gallant, nephew of Bill Murphy ('71) . . 132

Multiple Lenses, by Peter Loan ('72) 134

Lessons Learned, by Charlotte Cook (Lay Missioner ['92]) 139

Dick Ramsay, Priest and Prophet, by Frank Gerace ('64) 142

Transformation: A Cultural Odyssey, by Paul Newpower ('69) . . . 145

Roots and Wings, by Kevin Reid ('71) 154

For Joe Carney ('65), by the Joseph Hart Patrick Carney family,
  (Suga, Mark F., and Hana Marion Carney) 157

A Compelling Presence, by Paul Segall ('59) 160

Forever in My Dreams, by Lawrence D. Obrist ('69) 163

Primum Regnum Dei ...et Justicia Sua, by Dan Maloney ('60) 170

Endangered Species, by Al Stumph ('68) 175

Maryknoll to Africa: By a Different Course, by Tom
  Hinnebusch ('66) 179

Your Works Are Wonderful (Just As They Are), by Bill Murphy ('71) . 183

The Accidental Missionary, by John O'Connor ('72) 186

Blessed Am I, by Ev Charette ('72) 191

My Life and Maryknoll, by Charlie Lockwood ('71) 192

Adsum Domine, by Biff Jenney ('68) 195

Introduction

TURNS IN THE ROAD: COMPANIONS ON THE JOURNEY. That's the title Fr. Jack Sullivan, M.M., gave his essay that appears in this collection. With his permission we have chosen the same title for the entire publication. We believe this anthology will remind readers of how they too have approached and negotiated turns as they moved along their personal roads of life. We believe readers will also sense their own mentors and friends stepping along beside and in front of them in parallel to the authors' experiences. Indeed, the very Maryknoll community spirit that breathes life into these stories, poems, and essays will inspire imitation.

When the Society Alumni Coordinating Committee initiated this writing project to commemorate Maryknoll's first hundred years, there was discussion about what purpose the project might serve. Several ideas were generated. The content could serve as a complement to any official Society history, similar to the way Howard Zinn's *A People's History of the United States* complements the history narrative often taught in schools. It could provide an opportunity for those impacted by the Society, but not now serving as members, to explore and express the influence Maryknoll has had on the flow of their lives. It would provide insights into the growth of the authors over their lifetimes. The stories might help document the impact Maryknoll has had well beyond its traditional missionary work.

It turns out that this collection of writings serves those purposes and more. Most assuredly, the authors write about their Maryknoll experience but many do more than recount events. Several have taken a chance by reaching into their experiences to explore their pain, their doubts, and their joy.

Although it may, at times, have felt so to them, none of the authors traversed their life roads in isolation. Their Maryknoll community prevented that. Several writers have chosen to focus their stories on their companions on the road, those whose friendships have persisted for a lifetime. Some pay tribute to their mentors, teachers, or those at whose sides they served as missioners, while others tell how they learned invaluable lessons from those to whom they had been sent. Still others recount how they were pulled from feelings of isolation by the interventions of their fellow travelers along the Maryknoll Road.

All contributors to this collection traversed the Maryknoll Road as students, and, perhaps, as members of the Society, or as individuals whose lives were influenced by Society members. They grounded their compositions in the choices made as they arrived at turns in their road. Clearly, whether cruising along those sections smoothly paved or struggling for control along portions filled with potholes or finding their way through those parts that required the construction of new routes, these travelers experienced life-altering events. Their stories recount the ways their Maryknoll experience led them to interpret the road signs they encountered along the way.

As Jerry Murphy implies in his essay, "Reflections on the Relationships of the Maryknoll Society with Resigned Maryknollers," the fostering of a formal and continuing relationship between Maryknoll and its resigned members is unique among priestly Orders and Societies. All those traveling the Maryknoll Road have benefited by this relationship if only by experiencing the freedom to maintain the deep friendships that were birthed and nourished in the Society.

Jerry's essay pays tribute to those men who have been instrumental in growing this Maryknoll relationship. We also wish to honor them by acknowledging that this Centennial Writing Project would never have come about without their foresight and work over the past forty or fifty years.

There is one man, Fr. Robert Sheridan, M.M., whom we believe deserves special mention. For forty years prior to his death in 1987, RES, as many of us knew him, conducted a "personal apostolate" to former members of the Society. "Personal apostolate" was the phrase he chose to describe his work in a letter to Superior General Ray Hill in 1974. His *Chi Rho Newsletter* and

Tunc et Nunc newsletter ensured that contacts between Maryknoll-ers and the Society's former members would endure. And he maintained phone contact with many, whenever he and they felt that was needed. He did not hesitate to sit in a "former's" kitchen when invited. There he would share a cup of coffee, a bit of food, and the assurance that turns in the road and new paths taken did not erase years of friendships and collaborations.

We do not intend this collection to be an exercise in nostalgia, but rather, to incorporate a concept from Erik Erikson: this collection is a reflective integration of generativity and gratitude, a complementary history of the Maryknoll Society as it now begins its second century.

What would James Anthony and Thomas Frederick think or say if they could read this collection! A lot has changed in the past one hundred years and the next one hundred will certainly witness even more change for Maryknoll, the Church, and the world. Bishop Walsh and Father Price were great innovators in their day. We thank them for founding, and nourishing, the Society that has deeply affected our lives.

We especially thank the alumni contributors for taking the time and making the effort to reflect and write. In their company, we offer this anthology as our way of marking the Society's first one hundred years.

Al Stumph ('68)
Bill Murphy ('71)
Tom Fenton ('69)

Maryknoll, New York

Para los Pobres

Bob Maxwell ('56)

IN THE SPRING OF 1966, I was a Maryknoll priest stationed at the tiny village of San Miguel in northwestern Guatemala. This was in the Department (State) of Huehuetenango. This area is home to the Cuchamatanes Mountains, beautiful to look at but poor land for farming. The steep rocky mountainsides were densely forested.

This part of the country was inhabited almost entirely by Indians, descendants of the ancient Mayas, who had lived there for eons. Except for a very few who spoke Spanish, the people spoke the old Maya tongue. They were generally poor farming families who eked out a living on small ancestral plots of land. They wore the identical clothing that their forebears had worn for centuries, woven by the women from cotton or wool. The men had homemade sandals fashioned from leather and with soles cut from old automobile tires.

I had been called to a pastoral meeting of priests of the region. We were to gather at the parish in the village of Jacaltenango, which was a four-hour horseback ride from San Miguel. I rode over three mountains and forded the streams that flowed in the valleys. When I arrived in the village, I was a bit tired, and I'm sure my horse was too. So before going to meet the other priests, I stopped in the huge church that had been built by the Spanish Franciscans some three centuries beforehand. I wanted to rest a bit.

I was sitting alone on a bench near the center of the church when an Indian family slowly walked single-file up the aisle. The father walked first, followed by his wife, who was carrying a tiny baby. Close on her heels was a son about two years old. I was struck by the great dignity of the father. He was tall for an Indian and ramrod straight. He walked very slowly, looking straight ahead to the altar.

I was struck by the family's poverty. The father's homespun *capishay*, a kind of jacket, was faded and worn thin. The mother's long scarf, called a *rebozo*, was worn across one shoulder and under the other arm. It was tied in the front and cradled her baby on her back. Her *rebozo* was worn and was patched. The tiny lad, wearing his own small *capishay* and tattered trousers, followed. None of them wore shoes. Even in a population that knew no wealth, this family stood out as very poor. My heart went out to them, making me feel somewhat guilty for having ten dollars in my pocket.

The three of them went to the altar step and stood there in silence. The father seemed to be at prayer for perhaps two minutes. Then he turned and began to walk slowly back up the main aisle. His right arm hung down with his fingers pointing ahead, the way a beggar might look, hoping someone would place something in his hand.

His and my eyes met and I began to reach for my wallet. When he reached my bench he stopped. I saw that there were two pennies in his hand. I didn't know what to do. Slowly he reached out his hand and put the coins in my hand. He said simply, "Para los pobres." "For the poor."

All my being wanted to protest this gift. I ached to give him my ten dollars. But at the same time I knew that my money would defile that sacred moment.

Then they quietly walked to the door and out of the church.

❏

Bob and Liz Maxwell are retired and living in Cincinnati, Ohio.

Reflections on the Relationships of the Maryknoll Society with Resigned Maryknollers

Jerry Murphy ('58)

IT IS TRULY REMARKABLE that Maryknoll invites those of us who have left Maryknoll to join in the Centennial celebration of the Maryknoll Society (1911–2011). I know of no other priestly Order or Society that has fostered a formal and continuing relationship with resigned members as does Maryknoll. In order to understand how this phenomenon came about, I spent much time reviewing the reams of documents in my files from the early 1970s and, as a result, wish to pay tribute to some of the great men whose vision created the foundation for this enduring and healthy relationship that exists to this day.

Prompted by one of the 1972 Chapter Recommendations to "explore collaboration with former Maryknollers," Superior General Ray Hill, in a 1974 Christmas letter to former Maryknollers, invited interest toward a dialogue with Maryknoll. As a result, several resigned Maryknollers, wishing to pursue the meaning of this invitation, arranged meetings with Vicar General Joe Glynn and Secretary General Bill McIntyre. In the meantime, some of these same resigned Maryknollers were independently forming an organization in the hope of formally establishing various ministries for former priests and nuns that might also in some way be a viable response to Maryknoll's invitation to dialogue. The organization was called Maryknoll-in-Diaspora.

In 1977, Superior General Ray Hill, in a Christmas letter, once again expressed an interest in a formal dialogue with resigned Maryknollers. Maryknoll-in-Diaspora worked hard at reaching out to many resigned Maryknollers scattered throughout the country as to their collective interest in a dialogue with Maryknoll. In February 1978, at a pivotal meeting at the NYC 39th St. Maryknoll House with Vicar General Joe Glynn and some resigned Maryknollers, we were advised to develop a platform or plan to serve as a base for dialogue with the Society. In this regard, meetings of resigned Maryknollers were held in several regions throughout the year 1978. As a result, during the fall 1978 General Chapter, one of the Chapter delegates, John Harper ('75), arranged an informal meeting with Chapter delegates, at which a group of resigned Maryknollers made a presentation for the Chapter deliberations, emphasizing communication, collaboration, and cooperation. The presentation covered several points, viz., value of formers' years of service, potential contribution toward future Maryknoll mission activity, the need for a joint committee of current and resigned Maryknollers, and the possibility of a pension/severance plan. This resulted in a "Chapter Recommendation" to pursue dialogue with resigned Maryknollers. A number of resigned men gave of their time and energy toward creating a dialogue with the Society. However, at the forefront of this effort were Gregory Rienzo ('58), Raymond F. Kelly ('58), Gerry Grudzen ('67), Paul D'Arcy ('46), Ron DuBois ('63), and Jerry Murphy ('58).

Toward this end, Vicar General Jack Halbert ('59) met with a couple of resigned Maryknollers, and formal joint meetings between the Society and resigned Maryknollers began in August 1979 and continue to the present time.

The above paragraphs are deliberately only a brief sketch of the origin of the enduring relationship of the Society and its resigned members. There are many individuals both of the active Maryknollers and resigned members deserving a tribute for their combined efforts in creating a relationship of mutual respect. In my opinion, were it not for Superior General Ray Hill's vision toward creating a unity with resigned Maryknollers through dialogue, followed up by Joe Glynn and Bill McIntyre and later through the tireless efforts of Vicar General Jack Halbert, it is unlikely the mutual bonding and respectful relationship that exists today would have come about. Another giant who worked assiduously in the early 1980s at fostering open communication with both actives and resigned Maryknollers was Bob Sheridan. He authored the *Chi Rho Newsletter* and his famous *Tunc et Nunc* newsletter that were literally a who's who of names and events mailed out to over 800 active and resigned Maryknollers.

Of the three C's (communication, cooperation, collaboration), which were the main objectives of a formal dialogue between the active and resigned Maryknollers, perhaps the Joint Committee was most successful in the first two C's. Initiation of the *Interchange* periodic newsletter, whose editors have been Richard Armstrong ('59) and Tom Fenton ('69), became the vehicle for significantly improving communications and thereby created an avenue for better cooperation between active and resigned members. Establishing a Chi Rho Fund to assist people in a sundry of dire circumstances is also a notable product of the Joint Committee, as well as other innumerable benefits resulting from the Joint Committee forum, i.e., ordination reunions, Job Bank, picnics at Maryknoll, introduction of an internet *Interchange* listserv to foster discussions and sharing of information among the active and resigned members, etc.

What in the early seventies was a tenuous relationship between active and resigned Maryknollers marked by mistrust and strained attitudes has, over the years, through dialogue and open communications, developed into a healthy, mutually respectful relationship. I am eternally proud and grateful to be a Maryknoller.

❏

Jerome ("Jerry") Murphy and his Korean wife, Theresa, are retired and currently live in Newark, Del. They have three children and six grandchildren. Jerry entered Maryknoll at Glen Ellyn in 1949, after graduating from Bishop Loughlin High School. He was ordained at Maryknoll in 1958 and assigned to Korea. He served in the Inchon Diocese until September 1968. During that time, from 1964 to 1965, Jerry studied Mandarin Chinese at Yale University. After leaving Maryknoll, he worked for the State of New Jersey for 27 years, from 1969 to 1996, retiring as assistant director of Medicaid Agency. He then became a long-term care consultant from 1996 to 2005.

Five More Years

James C. O'Connor ('63)

WHEN I WAS IN THE EIGHTH GRADE at the Gesu Parish grammar school, Fr. Bob Sheridan spoke to the whole school. We were assembled in the gymnasium, standing heel to toe. Later that month I took a Dexter Avenue bus to the Maryknoll house and introduced myself. That September I enrolled in Sacred Heart Seminary high school.

Four years later, I traveled to the Venard in Scranton, Pa. That was September of 1943. Some of my high school classmates, when they finished high school did not continue in the seminary then in Detroit—where the Seminary included four years of high school and four years of college. The major seminary for the diocese was in Cincinnati, Ohio. Those who did not continue were either drafted into the army or volunteered for the Navy or Marines. One of my friends, Jim Mason, joined the Marines and ended up as a machine gunner in a dive-bomber. He got to China before any of us, being stationed after the war near Shanghai. The other class-mate, whose name I can't remember now, was killed in one of the island invasions.

After two years at the Venard, I moved on to the major seminary in Ossining, N.Y., where I completed college and went to Bedford, Mass. for the novitiate. As I look back on that time, I think I would have been better educated if I had remained in Detroit for the four years of college at Sacred Heart Seminary. The reason being that the course of studies in Detroit was more complete, the teachers better equipped. As it was at the Venard, Maryknoll had accepted students from all kinds of high schools and so the mixture of ac-complishments varied considerably. For example, Fr. Joe Hahn taught physics. As far as I remember the classes were a repeat of the physics I had in high school—the same for Latin and Spanish.

I moved on to Maryknoll, N.Y., to finish college and then went to the novitiate in Bedford, Mass. Fr. Joe Donnelly was the novice master, I think, or was he in charge the second time in the novitiate. After two years more of theology, I took a break and stepped out. That's when I joined the Michigan Air National Guard. That happened relatively quickly because the rector (Fr. Comber) did not waste any time advising the draft board of my new status. The National Guard was soon called to active duty. I enjoyed those years in the Guard. My time was spent for the most part in Arizona and also in Louisiana for flight training.

Returning home, having been released from active duty, I took up the construction business and financed by my Dad, I began building single-family houses, which I sold one by one. After some years, the class that was ordained in either 1953 or 1954, had a reunion at the promotion house in Detroit, where Fr. Jack King was in charge. Pete Halligan invited me to join the group and there I met many of the former classmates, now priests, whom I knew from the olden days. It caused me to take another look at where I was headed and later that year I called Fr. Jack King and asked him about the possibility of rejoining Maryknoll. He talked to Fr. Comber (the superior general by that time) and when I called Fr. Comber the next day he said that there was no problem, but that I would have to repeat the novitiate. He apologized, saying that there was nothing he could do because it was Canon Law. So I repeated the novitiate, joined the 3rd theology class, taught by my former classmatem, Fr. Ed Malone. I was ordained in June of 1963. Today the picture of that class should be still hanging in the Main corridor at the Knoll.

Off to Bolivia in August by steamer and about two weeks later we docked at the Peruvian port next to Lima. The group of us spent the night at the Center House, and next morning we were hustled off on the bus to Bolivia.

My Maryknoll life on the foreign missions began there in the Cochabamba Language School, where after about 4 months, I was assigned to Montaro, where I became an assistant to Fr. Gus Kircher, the pastor. My predecessor, Fr. Bill Kruegler, was killed while standing in the door of the old rectory by someone from the

Maryknoll Novitiate, Bedford, Massachusetts

bar next door, who was upset because Bill had been complaining about the noise. A crowd gathered in the plaza immediately and dragged the fellow across the street and hung him from a tree in the Plaza Central de Montaro.

Montaro was a town that would have fit right in with the 1890s American West, where herds of cattle were trailed up from the Beni for a hundred miles or more on their way to Santa Cruz, the department capital. When you sent the cook out to buy some meat, she didn't get it at the butcher shop in the form of a steak or a rib. She went down a couple blocks to where the cattle had been gathered for a rest. At that point some were slaughtered and the meat was cut in strips and flung over a clothesline. As soon as it hit the line it was covered with flies.

I was there for at least two years. Frank Gerace arrived during my second year. Since he already spoke Spanish (picked up on the street in Harlem, I guess) he skipped language school.

Dick Ramsay, who had been assigned to Cochabamba, was interested in a change and when I heard about it I went to Fr. Gordon Fritz, the regional superior. Gordon had a custom of visiting all the missions in Bolivia at least twice a year, mainly, as we observed, to make sure that the places were kept neat and clean and no scraps of paper were blowing around.

Dick and I changed places and I went to Cochabamba. I found myself at home there and thrived.

Summing up.

How am I who I am as a result of my Maryknoll experience? I feel that since I spent almost one-half of my life involved in some way with Maryknoll, I gained the friendship of many Maryknollers— some very close—and they (those still living) are still my close friends whom I value highly.

What choices in your life did Maryknoll influence? First, where I went to school; second where I met my future wife. Speaking Spanish helped me get my job after returning to the states. When I look back, I am surprised at how little thought I seemed to give to getting a job and making a living. For some reason I thought there would be no problem. But when I think about the skills that I learned in Maryknoll, the only one that was useful was my ability to speak pretty good Spanish.

So for now—basta! Could I write more? Probably. Thanks for opportunity to think about my time in Maryknoll.

❏

"Five more years" is what Jim says to his wife of 41 years, Mary. "But no guarantee." On retiring in the 1990s, they bought a 10-acre apple orchard in Sonoma County, Calif., and converted it into a vineyard. The lower half was planted in Chardonnay grapes and the upper went to Pinot Noir grapes. Jim sells the Chardonnay and crushes the Pinot to make wine under the "O'Connor Vineyards" label. Jim and Mary's daughter, Sara, has a BA from UC Berkeley and a law degree from the University of Santa Clara. She and her husband, also an attorney, have a son, 12, and a daughter, 8. Mary wonders, "At 70, he planted a vineyard. At 80, he started producing wine for his own label. What will he do at 90?"

Maryknoll's Influence in My Life

Joseph J. Fahey ('67)

O N JUNE 23, 1958, I received a letter from Fr. Carroll I. Quinn, M.M., that would change my life forever. It began, "Welcome to Maryknoll!" Fr. Quinn stated, "I am confident that you will put your whole heart and mind to this serious work of your priestly and foreign mission training, since nothing on this earth is more important." Along with about 60 other robust young seminarians, I entered Glen Ellyn and began my first year of college. I stayed, finished GE, Novitiate, and left in III Theology at Maryknoll, N.Y., in my eighth year of seminary studies. Those simple facts sound so cold, but those years in Maryknoll were among the happiest of my life and they have had a profound influence on my personal values and career. I met some of the most wonderful men in the world and still count many Maryknollers as dear friends. Every time I visit the Knoll, I am again filled with a warm feeling and I again feel at home.

Through Maryknoll, I came to understand the Christian vocation as one centered in the quest for peace through justice. Perhaps the most influential book I read in the seminary was Bonhoeffer's *The Cost of Discipleship*. In that book, he makes the distinction between "cheap" and "costly" grace. The cheap grace is the grace of the status quo that accepts things as they are and views the Christian vocation primarily in secular terms. Consequently, the Church has little to say to the world and survives quite nicely in a world of capitalism and war. Bonhoeffer lived out "costly" grace and resisted with his own life the terror of the fascists of his time. Through him (and, of course, many other seminary influences), I came to see that the Christian vocation was one that must transform the values of the world and create—in the words of the *Compendium of the Social Doctrine of the Church*—a "civilization of love." Love, of course, that is rooted in social justice for all.

I began teaching theology at Manhattan College in 1966 and, frankly, was not very good at all. It took me almost ten years before I felt comfortable standing before a college class (getting a PhD helped, of course). I was always attracted to moral theology and, fortunately, I developed early on a course on "Contemporary Moral Issues," which I still teach. In my first year or two at Manhattan, some students suggested that I teach a course on peace and I reluctantly did so because I didn't know much more than the Just War theory. But then I remembered Pope John's *Pacem in Terris,* which I had read in novitiate in 1963, and that became the blueprint for my course and, indeed, for my career. I was strongly influenced by the Maryknoll focus on global issues, and that background contributed mightily to my courses, scholarship, and activism. I visited the Catholic Worker often in those early days and conversations with Dorothy Day helped me to focus on the radical call of the Gospel that is the foundation for peace. My peace course and several others led eventually to the formation of a BA in peace studies, the first at a Catholic college in the country. (There are now over 300 degree-granting peace studies programs in the world.)

In the summers of 1969 and 1970, I had the great honor of working at the Christophers in New York City. I saw Maryknoll Fathers Jim Keller and Dick Armstrong every day and was deeply honored when Fr. Keller (we called him "JK") would take notes on something I had said with the ever-increasing shaking hands due to Parkinson's. I wrote several pamphlets for the Christophers and I remember the day when Dick and JK told me they were going to put my name on them both to show that an academic had written them and, I strongly suspect, to divert some of the flack that would surely come (it did!) to me. *Peace, War and the Christian Conscience* sold well over a million copies, and I was thrilled to learn that it helped so many GI's get CO status during Vietnam. The Christophers was, of course, a Maryknoll project (although I later learned that there were some in the Society who didn't think JK's project should have been undertaken at all!). But I have carried the positive, hopeful message of the Christophers with me wherever I have gone. "Better to light one candle than to curse the darkness" seems trite to some, but it is just the message that the negative, narcissistic world of Rush Limbaugh and the professional pessimists need. It was at the Christophers that I developed an interest in my favorite "heretic," Pelagius, and eventually learned that he was wrongly condemned by Augustine and others in large part because he didn't at all buy into Augustine's then novel—and in my view—profoundly unchristian doctrine of original sin. JK confessed to being a "semi-Pelagian," but he did so with that sly smile on his face. To me, he was a full-blown Pelagian who believed in the inherent goodness of every person. (By the way, don't get me wrong, I know from bitter personal experience what it means to be a sinner, but I reject the idea that I was born that way!)

In the early 1970s, I was one of the founders of Pax Christi USA (with Dorothy Day, Eileen Egan, Gordon Zahn, Tom Gumbleton, and so many other wonderful people) and I served in several capacities, including general secretary and member of the international movement. My involvement in Pax Christi took me all over the world. I even made several trips behind the Iron Curtain to meet with church people and professors to explore our common humanity. I also had the good fortune to work with other Pax Christi scholars and activists on drafts for the U.S. bishops' 1983 peace pastoral.

I have always been an "activist" professor, due in large part to my Maryknoll training. In recent years, I have become quite active with labor unions. Just a few years ago I founded Catholic Scholars for Worker Justice to offer the voice of scholars who are committed to Catholic social teaching in support of workers at both Catholic and secular institutions. I also, along with several other faculty members, recently started a BA program in labor studies at Manhattan College, and it is a joy to end my career with yet another missionary venture in academe! All of my work can be traced to my Maryknoll training, and I am deeply grateful for those wonderful years.

I also had a very rare opportunity for one who had left the Society. I taught as an adjunct prof at the Knoll for about ten years in the 1970s and 1980s. Through those years, I met a younger generation of Maryknollers and worked with some wonderful former professors like Bill Frazier, Bill McCarthy, and Jack Keegan. I also taught in Jack Rich's Mission Renewal Program and met many missioners from other missionary communities, both women and men. I also got to know the Maryknoll Sisters, since I did some work with them especially through Annette Mulrey. Even though I have always loved my undergraduates at Manhattan, I must admit that the most rewarding teaching I ever did was at the Knoll and in the Mission Renewal Program. I experienced eager students, who wanted to know everything they could about, for example, Gene Sharp's 198 ways of nonviolent resistance and the Church's teaching on social justice. Many have stayed in touch, and I learned a good deal about nonviolence "on the ground" in mission countries. It was, indeed, a rare privilege and one I shall cherish always. The *Maryknoll Spiritual Directory* defined a missioner as a "man with a message who mixes with men" (today, of course, we would say "person" and "people") and that defines those wonderful people I met in those years.

But above all, Maryknoll is people. I can honestly say that the Maryknollers are the finest men (and women) I have ever met. I think it was James E. Walsh, who said that the Maryknoll spirit was "charity" and that defines for me the Maryknoll men I have known. I could mention scores of names that easily come to mind when I think of the Maryknoll spirit...men like Gerry Kelly, Steve

Maryknoll College, Glen Ellyn, Illinois

Fleischer, Leo Shea, Chris Brickley, Bill Donnelly, Paul Maguire, Pete Chabot, Denny Mahon, Tom Marti, Pat Murphy, and some wonderful professors—from Norb Fleckenstein, George Putnam, Tom Wilcox, and Bill Frazier through Joe Grassi—but this short list doesn't do justice to all the great guys I have met. When I think of them to this day, I experience an inner joy.

In conclusion, I say a profound word of thanks for my Maryknoll training and for the vision that it gave me to pursue a life dedicated, as much as I could, to making the world a better place for all. But above all, I say thanks to all the great guys I have met through the years. When I walk the corridors of the Knoll today, I occasionally close my eyes and once again hear the laughter that filled that wonderful house and I see the smiling faces of young men who believed there was a world to be won for the Reign of God on earth. When I visit "God's Acre" and see the names of the great men who have gone before us, I pledge to them to continue Maryknoll's mission in and for the world. Although I have chosen to live my Maryknoll call to mission outside the Society, I am, and always will be, a Maryknoller.

❏

Joe lives in White Plains, NY, and can be reached at josephjfahey @gmail.com.

Swings and Roundabouts

Robert Connolly ('79)

WE HAVE AN EXPRESSION IN IRELAND asserting that in life what you "gain on the swings, you lose on the round-abouts." Apparently, the Irish are not proponents of the "win-win" scenario, believing that for every positive there is usually a negative. And so it was with my Maryknoll experience.

I entered Maryknoll in 1965 at the end of the junior seminary days with the China stories of Fr. Robert Greene, RIP, encouraging me to embrace the exciting life of a missionary priest. My grandfather was a financial advisor to Fr. James Drought in the early days of the Society; supporting Maryknoll was always an important part of our family life. In retrospect, it was a bit much for a 14-year-old pre-pubescent boy, but at the time, that was the way things were done, and I could not have been happier during my Chesterfield days.

I was surrounded by young men who apparently shared similar backgrounds and aspirations. I lived a structured life from morning prayers to "magnum silentium," which ensured that there was little extra time for getting into trouble. The faculty consisted of well-educated and dedicated teachers, and with a student-faculty ratio of about four to one, it was impossible to get lost in the shuffle. The class work was challenging, and with mandatory study halls, avoiding the work was not an option. As a result, I acquired an exceptionally strong educational foundation that made my subsequent education, up to and including law school at Notre Dame, much easier.

A few years after leaving, during my final examinations in my first year of law school, I was asked to translate the following torts maxim: "Cuius est solum eius est usque ad coelum et ad inferos." Thanks to my Latin teacher, Andy Balistreri, I recognized enough words to accurately translate the phase. I later asked Professor Charles Rice why he had included so obscure a reference. He said that the question was his gift to those of us with a classic education. Unquestionably, my education at Maryknoll was a swing.

The same also could be said about the range of extracurricular activities that were available at Chesterfield. Paging through my copy of the final yearbook, *Quest*, it is hard to believe that there were over 20 clubs, teams, and organizations, excluding sports, for a student body of 80. Since there seemed to be at least a dozen members in each organization, friendship and cooperation were developed on many levels. As for sports, I was not the most physically gifted athlete to ever grace the halls of Maryknoll, but I was enthusiastic and a quick study, embracing soccer and baseball, where my vertical challenge was not a major drawback. Like our manager, Mr. John Murray, I was a catcher. He taught me intricacies of the game that I later passed on to my nieces and nephews. I learned more about soccer from Mr. Edwin Jordan, who coached our inter-school team, than I can possibly recount. Clearly, I would not have been appointed the head soccer coach at Notre Dame

Chapel, Maryknoll High School, Chesterfield, Missouri

were it not for the lessons learned from his instruction. Summarily, the social, extracurricular, and athletic opportunities Maryknoll presented were also significant swings.

There were, of course, also roundabouts, the most obvious of which were addressed by the Society's decision to close the minor seminary and, ultimately, the college seminary at Glen Ellyn. When these closures were announced, I was particularly disappointed, undoubtedly because I was having too much fun to see the bigger picture. After Chesterfield closed in 1969, I reported to Glen Ellyn, where I finished my secondary education in a local high school before entering the college seminary in 1970. When Glen Ellyn closed in 1971, I decided that these closures were God's gentle way of nudging me away from the priesthood, so I moved on to Notre Dame, confident that she was unlikely to abandon me. Fortunately for Maryknoll, some of my classmates, like Fr. John McAuley, who in our school days was my totally unbiased source whenever I was making a particularly outrageous statement, did not hear God's voice in the same way I did. In fact, he was closed out of the Venard as well as Chesterfield and Glen Ellyn but still found his way back.

It was only years later that the roundabout inherent in a minor seminary education became apparent. While other young men my age were taking their first tentative steps toward what might ultimately develop into relationships, marriage, and a family, I had dedicated myself to Our Lady and had no time for even the most innocent flirtations. Not that I didn't face my share of temptations, including working with beautiful southern girls on a few "mission" trips I took with Will Ament, Andy Balistreri, and Ron DuBois to teach catechism in Mississippi. At the time, however, I was serious about my vocation, so I avoided what I deemed to be occasions of sin. This roundabout was to haunt me for some years to come.

I suppose it didn't help that when I finally parted company with Maryknoll, the University of Notre Dame had not yet embraced coeducation, so the next stop on my educational journey was a school with five thousand testosterone-filled young men and only a few women in sight. Rather than entering a swing to make up for my Maryknoll roundabout by trying to compete for the few available women, I chose to embrace my soccer and studies, which further retarded my social growth as it related to women. It was only when I entered law school that, for the first time, I was in an environment where men and women participated equally in an educational and social environment. Although I got on very well with all my classmates, I was woefully naive about reading the signals that apparently emanated from my female classmates, nor did I have a clue about sending my own. As a result, my one attempt at establishing a bit of a relationship was met with those words that chill the soul of anyone who fancies a girl, "You're just like a brother to me."

A few years after graduating from law school, I met the love of my life. She was a dark-haired Irish beauty, a few years younger than I, very bright, with sparkling eyes and an ability to laugh at herself and the world in general. Although she lived in Ireland, I traveled a bit, as did she, so we encountered each other off and on until she realized that, as they say over here, "I had a bit of a *grá* (or love) for her," which obviously was not reciprocated. As a result, I got the other line that also chills the heart of anyone who fancies a girl, "You're like my best friend, but I don't think of you in romantic terms."

Apparently, I was accomplished at being a good brother. With eight siblings, that was not a surprise. I was also good at being a friend, undoubtedly one of the Maryknoll swings, but the roundabout was that I never quite figured out what one says or does to be attractive as a potential romantic partner, which leads to the biggest swing/roundabout of them all.

A couple of years ago, Andy Balistreri and his wife Sheila were on a European cruise and stopped in to visit my wife and me in Dublin. Since I hadn't seen Andy in nearly forty years, I was thrilled that he contacted me and even more delighted that we were able to get together for an afternoon. Of course, we discussed our common Maryknoll experiences, catching up on the decades that had passed and on the many names that had receded from our collective memories. I mentioned that I did not regret one moment of my Maryknoll years, and I specifically recalled a formation retreat that I attended in the last days of Glen Ellyn. One of the themes of the retreat was that by living an exemplary life, a Maryknoller's task is to make a Buddhist a better Buddhist, a philosophy that I have never forgotten, although my application might fall short now and again. My mother-in-law claims that I am a dangerous person because I remember far too much, but I trust that does not apply to my Maryknoll experiences.

I asked Andy why it was that so many of the young priests that I knew and respected from my seminary days had been laicized and ultimately married. One part of his response made perfect sense, while the other initially took me by surprise. In the first instance, he suggested that one could live an exemplary life, effectively making a Buddhist a better Buddhist, without being ordained to the priesthood. This realization caused many young priests to seek other paths. Although I understood the comment, one might be left wondering if the Maryknoll journey, leading through education and formation, was directed toward an unnecessary goal, i.e., ordination. Of course, the ordained priesthood plays a vital role in the propagation of the faith and the continuation of the Church, a role that cannot be understated, because that is how the actual message of the gospel is shared. However, in terms of the ethos of Maryknoll, Christ said in St. John's gospel, "By this will all men know that you are my disciples, if you have love for one another." Apparently, Maryknollers are created in the formation and not in the ordination, and I was privileged to experience at least a small part of that formation.

Andy's second comment took me by surprise. He said that many former priests married because one thing Maryknoll excelled at was making good husbands and fathers. That was certainly an aspect of my Maryknoll experience that I had not considered, but on reflection it was obvious. Since the vast majority of people ultimately marry, living an exemplary life would typically include commitment to a life partner. Most Maryknollers, including half-Maryknollers like myself, undoubtedly came from strong family units so their early lives were founded in love and support. An education and formation that included respect for all people and a dedication to Our Lady would certainly provide the ideal scenario for a committed relationship and, ideally, create a template for a loving and supportive husband and father.

That commitment to marriage necessarily reflected all the practical skills learned during manual labor, whether in the kitchen, the laundry, the garage, or when applying a mop and bucket. Being handy, I discovered, is an attractive feature in a life partner. Few men, or women, who spent years appreciating the need to partici-pate in the mundane tasks of living in a community, would be likely to become couch potatoes when there was work to be done. Similarly, living in a community requires a more selfless commit-ment to the whole, which often includes subordinating personal interests and preferences to those of the unit. As Andy remarked, taken as a whole, Maryknoll formation and education provided an ideal foundation for creating an excellent husband and father.

My life's journey was clearly blessed with the swing of a Mary-knoll experience that would help me lead an exemplary life and, hopefully, make me a good husband and father. Unfortunately, the ultimate roundabout was that as a result of pursuing a vocation to the ordained priesthood, I hadn't a clue about establishing a ro-mantic relationship that might result in my becoming a good husband and father. On the other hand, Maryknoll also provided me with a "can do" attitude. So with a bit of prayer, patience, per-sistence, and perseverance, I find myself living in Dublin, writing, practicing law, and married to the love of my life. Apparently, when we reconnected nearly twenty years after parting company, Pamela decided that I had improved with age. Undoubtedly, Mary-knoll provided me far more swings than roundabouts. Thank you, Maryknoll.

❑

Robert resides in Dublin, Ireland, with his wife Pamela, a secondary school teacher. He has written a few books, including: *If Walls Could Talk: Great Irish Castles Tell Their Stories; The Legends: Beginnings;* and *The Rise and Fall of the Irish Pub.* In his day job, he is a practicing solicitor, primarily representing pubs and restaurants.

Marrying a Former Priest

Florence McGuire
(wife of P. Thomas McGuire ['67])

I WAS BORN IN TSINGDAO, CHINA, a place famous for Tsingdao beer, during the Japanese occupation of the city. My parents brought my three brothers and me to Hong Kong before the founding of the People's Republic of China. We grew up in Hong Kong and I started my education at Heep Yunn Girls' School near our home in Kowloon. I graduated there and entered New Asia College, the Chinese University of Hong Kong, just across the street from Heep Yunn on Farm Road.

Heep Yunn is an Anglican Church school; we had Bible classes all through 12 years. But I was not baptized in the Anglican Church. I joined the Girl Scout troop of St. Rose of Lima Catholic Girls' School and went to "observe mass" with the other girl scouts at St. Theresa Catholic Church. I liked the Mass even though I did not understand a word of the Latin.

I was seriously injured in a car accident during the first semester in college. While unconscious, at the request of my Catholic aunt, Fr. Orlando, an Italian Catholic priest from St. Theresa parish, baptized me as a Catholic in the hospital. When I regained consciousness, I had a profound conversion to the saving Lord, Jesus Christ, who brought me back to life. But with no understanding of what it meant to be a Catholic, I began to practice my faith in an Anglican Church.

During my college years, I learned how to teach the Cantonese dialect to the Maryknoll Sisters at the hospital in Wong Tai Sin near my home. We had moved there after my high school graduation and my two older brothers went to the United States to study.

I was glad that I could teach the Sisters to speak Cantonese, so they could help the poor in Hong Kong. At that time, the Sisters still wore the old habit, which impressed me very much. They looked like goddesses to me.

After I graduated from New Asia College, I was hired as a language instructor at the New Asia Yale-in-China Chinese language center. The students were from different countries and various different missions. During the late 1960s, few Sisters wore the old habit and some priests did not wear the white collar. The young priests looked like movie stars. Teaching them to speak Cantonese was like a "holy job" to me. I was preparing them for their mission to help the refugees from Mainland China and build the church in Hong Kong. I felt what I did was also a help to those in need. I enjoyed my teaching job very much and, on weekends, brought the language students, mostly the missionaries, to the little Hong Kong islands for outings, swimming, and Chinese meals in the evening. It was an opportunity for me to introduce them to Chinese culture and etiquette.

One day, I heard that two of the priest students, Herb Pierson

Maryknoll College, Glen Ellyn, Illinois

('68) and Al Stumph ('68), were leaving the priesthood to get married. I thought: "How could that happen?" Tom McGuire ('67), one of my priest students, told me that priests are also human, and they can have all sorts of reasons for leaving their active ministry as priests. Oh????? I then realized that priests and Sisters are not gods or goddesses, but human just like everyone else.

I continued to teach Cantonese and also visit Tom McGuire at his parish from time to time. One day, he told me that he was leaving the priesthood and asked me if I would marry him. I was a little puzzled, because I considered Tom a very good friend whom I could trust.

I was not thinking of getting married, for I had no boyfriends. I enjoyed being single. One of my friends told me that I dressed more like a "nun" than my Sister students. I believed that God had a plan for me and that He would show me what that plan was. So I prayed, talked with my Anglican pastor, and my parents. I enjoyed being with Tom McGuire and, if I were to get married, Tom was someone I would like to marry. It became very clear to me that marrying Tom was the plan God had for me.

After we married, it turned out that there was a small group of former priests married to Chinese women in Hong Kong, so we formed a "club" and had many gatherings. The husbands continued to share their faith and serve the needs of the people in Hong Kong. It seemed to me that they continued to carry out their mission in Hong Kong.

After being married to Tom McGuire for 39 years and meeting many couples like us, I have noticed that former priests are kind, educated, and talented people. Most of them continue to work in positions to help people. They still carry out Jesus' command to love others. They have a deep faith in Christ. They are very caring people and sometimes a little silly and nutty, but, most of all, they are good husbands. I thank God for this very good plan for me.

❑

Tom McGuire ('67), living a nomadic life style with his wife, Florence, is better known as a full-time RV-er, one who lives in a recreation vehicle. We sold our old family home in Detroit to our son, John. Our daughter bought a house in Chicago. We split the stuff from the house with them and now we are free to live day-to-day as it comes. I am retired from ministry in the Catholic Church and now active in support of the Catholic Church in China. We are blessed!

Turns in the Road: Companions on the Journey

John Sullivan, M.M. ('60)

THE SOCIETY WILL BE "what its members make it." A plaque on the wall in the main corridor of the Maryknoll Minor Seminary (the "Venard") enshrined words something like those when I first joined the future ranks of the Maryknoll Society alumni as a high school junior in 1949. These centennial sentiments and thoughts for the future of the Maryknoll Society flow from my continuing journey in the Society expression of the Maryknoll Movement. I have been part of a Maryknoll Society "in process" still being made by its members, the Maryknoll Movement and the Church in the United States. I will try to describe briefly some of the surprising "turns in the road" during my 62-year Maryknoll journey, and the lifetime gifts received from companions along the way. These turns in the road and companions have made, and are still making my journey possible, challenging and life giving. I will end this reflection with some possible turns in the road ahead, and some dreams for the future of the Maryknoll Society, Movement and Church.

In 1949 I made my first "turn" in the road to Maryknoll by leaving a Brooklyn, N.Y., high school for the Venard. I was a "delayed vocation" since I joined my class in my junior year! All but three of my 35 classmates had entered the seminary right out of grammar school. The Maryknoll seminaries then were filling with an ever-increasing flow of young men from strong, ghetto-like Catholic parishes; we were mostly young students from Catholic high schools and some veterans from the schools of the Second World

34

War and later Korea. These were the years of first and lasting friendships with classmates and faculty, an initial time of feeling "at home" with Maryknoll personnel and our common missionary dream. Even though about one out of five seminarians in each class made it to ordination or Brother candidates to Final Oath, the Society by 1960 could and did boast of its 1250 priests and Brothers, and its hundreds of seminarians and dozens of Brother candidates. We were young in age then, with perhaps less than a dozen members over 65 years old! We all thought such growth was normal, and would go on forever.

Thirty-two of us were ordained in June 1960; we were considered a "small" class at the time. We received our first mission assignments; mine was to the Formosa Region, which included Hong Kong. The people and the Maryknollers of Hong Kong quickly became part of my life. We went out to the "missions" to spend the rest of our lives living and working in another culture, language, country, and church. I discovered the wider Maryknoll Family in shared ministries and concerns with the men of the Hong Kong and with the Maryknoll Sisters long established there. We all discovered Society, Church, and political currents and conflicts little spoken of or even known about during seminary days. My special challenge working with the Chinese people of Hong Kong was to discover that Cantonese language learning and frustration were to be life-long challenges with little personal prospect of ever being fully literate. My new companions were the people of the parishes in which I worked, and the other priests, Sisters and Brothers of the Hong Kong Region and Church.

The people of Hong Kong revealed God to me in unexpected ways; some friendships were formed that have continued throughout my life. I was challenged to be an initiator at regional and parish levels. Much by accident I found myself working as a peer partner for five years in a parish with a small group of Maryknoll Sisters who were far superior to me in life and mission experience. They welcomed me as their brother and friend; from them I learned about teamwork and partnership even before I knew those terms. I began my lifelong experience of having real sisters and friends in Maryknoll.

My next major "turn" was to be elected the first regional superior of the newly established region of Hong Kong in 1968.

Vatican II hopes and aspirations were translated into polarized positions during these years. As one of the older of the younger men in the Formosa Region I had worked with the majority of the men in Hong Kong for a new Society Region. With the establishment of the Hong Kong Region in 1968, I found myself "unanimously" elected, i.e., two thirds of the men were fully supportive, one third fully opposed! We struggled to give life to the concepts of collegiality, subsidiarity, and consensus. We puzzled and grieved as our Maryknoll friends and brothers began to leave the Region, the priesthood, and Maryknoll. I formed friendships with the Chinese bishop of Hong Kong, and many of its Church and other leaders and worked more closely with Maryknoll Sisters and other Chinese and western Sisters of Hong Kong. I learned much more of the global Maryknoll through inter-regional and Society meetings.

A Maryknoll Sister competently helped me set up a regional office and kept me from being buried in a pre-computer and internet paper avalanche. These five years or so of deep involvement in Regional and Society concerns no doubt insulated me from some of the tensions being faced by many Society members at that time. I found myself walking with some of them as counselor and friends, seeking answers to their own questions about their future as priests and Brothers. In doing so it seems I was answering some of my own and felt even more committed to remain a Maryknoll priest.

Another major "turn" in the road took place in 1973 when I left Hong Kong, responding to an assignment to the Society Formation and Education Department as the Society's first full-time coordinator of the Overseas Training Program for its seminarians and Brothers. My new companions on the journey were professionally trained Society educators. This was my first in-depth contact with the Society in the United States and in other countries. I began attending and giving workshops, retreats, and seminars in the United States and continued traveling to do the same in many of the Maryknoll regions and other mission areas. During these years in the "FED" I started to work in collaboration with Maryknoll Sister Maria Rieckelman. She was a physician and psychiatrist with extensive mission experience. Gifted and creative Maryknoll Sisters worked with me during the expansion of the Overseas Training Program, especially Sister Johanna Murphy, who shared her organizational skills with me during these years. I found many new companions in the Society, in the Maryknoll Sisters Congregation, and among relatives and new acquaintances in the United States.

Lay ministry was one of my great interests while in the seminary; this interest grew and evolved in Hong Kong in work with local catechists and especially through involvement with the Young Christian Workers, who succeeded in helping me listen and begin "to see, judge, and act." I was one of the advocates of lay missioners at the Society's 1972 Chapter, as was Ray Hill who was later elected superior general at that Chapter. In January 1975 he asked me to continue and expand the Society's commitment to lay ministry by establishing the Lay Missioner Office and Program. My past, very positive experience of partnership with various Maryknoll Sisters and lay ministers encouraged me to set up this Program and Office in collaboration with the Sisters. I did this work with the full support of Ray Hill. Maryknoll Sister Mary Anne O'Donnell and I established the Maryknoll Lay Mission Office and Program as a collaborative joint project of both the Maryknoll Society and Congregation. We soon recruited former Glenmary lay missioner Chuck Lathrop to join us as a member of our coordination team. This team model of ministerial peers proved to be very fruitful and initially somewhat controversial to more traditional Maryknollers. These five years promoting the Maryknoll Lay Missioners within the Maryknoll Movement were a major turning point in my life as a Maryknoller.

An unexpected "turn" in the road took place in 1979 when new Society leadership affirmed the growth of the Maryknoll Lay Missioners, removed Mary Anne, Chuck and me, and replaced us with a lay team working more directly under their direction and with their full support. The Maryknoll Sisters continued as collaborators but were no longer considered to be co-sponsors of the whole Program. Mary Anne, Chuck, and I had been working to develop a lay organization that could be a full partner and peer to the Society and Maryknoll Sisters Congregation rather than associates of the clerical Society. However the Maryknoll Lay Missioners then became Associate Lay Missioners of the Society for the next fourteen years. In 1991 they finally became a more autonomous expression of the Maryknoll Movement. This very unexpected and painful "turn" of events led me to a new part of my Maryknoll journey through professional studies in pastoral counseling. I had hoped for such studies when I left Hong Kong in 1973. I took a degree in pastoral counseling and subsequently worked at Maryknoll, N.Y., doing continuing education ministry for two more years.

It was while doing this continuing education ministry that I became more involved in global "ministry to ministers" with Maria Rieckelman. We began "mission journeys" of some six months or so and continued doing so for nearly 25 years. We were able to travel many times to be with Maryknoll priests, Brothers, Sisters, Lay Missioners, Affiliates, and other missioners and mission personnel all over the world. We only went to serve them when invited and in response to their expressed needs; we companioned Maryknoll missioners "on their own turf," in the midst of their mission ministries and lives. We also worked together guiding Maryknoll reflection and pilgrimage retreats in Israel and Palestine. The fact that we were both mission experienced Maryknollers, a Sister and priest with professional training in mission spirituality, psychology and counseling opened the doors to the hearts and minds of many Maryknollers. And the Maryknoll Society has made this friendship and collaboration possible and acceptable for some two thirds of my Maryknoll life. This partnership ministry continues up to the present with necessary adaptation demanded by our own aging and energy. This "turn" in the road with its discovery of a true collaborator, friend, and companion on the journey, has no doubt contributed most to my mission vision and creative energy, and has empowered me to continue on the road as a Maryknoll priest missioner.

The development of and demand for this partnership "ministry to ministers" brought me to another major "turn" in my life, a return to the Hong Kong Region in 1982. Society leadership thought it best for me to return to my former region and perhaps continue ministry to ministers there, and from there, rather than from the Maryknoll Center in New York. I returned to Hong Kong as to a new mission assignment. This British Crown Colony was a new place moving toward assimilation into the Peoples' Republic of China, to what was later to be called a "Special Administrative Region." It was a wealthier and more intense place for its 4 million residents. I returned to minister to ministers and secondarily to do direct mission ministry in the parishes and be involved in regional and church administration.

In fact the Hong Kong Region turned out to be an ideal site for the continuation of my partnership ministry with Maria, who had had previous mission experience in both Korea and Hong Kong. I continued this ministry among local mission personnel and found many new companions among the priests, Sisters, ministers, service professionals of Hong Kong. Maria and I occasionally ministered together to local Church groups, and continued responding to invitations from all over the mission world with the total support of both Society and Congregational leadership. I helped out in the region, in the diocese and parishes for about six months of each year, and co-ministering with Maria in many mission areas for the other six months. She would come from the States and I from Hong Kong to offer our services as requested. This arrangement proved to be logistically simple. It was especially effective since we were more easily welcomed as invited guests to the regions rather than as official representatives sent by and answerable to Maryknoll, N.Y., offices and departments. My last seven years in the Hong Kong Region were spent living and ministering in a Kowloon parish, which I had helped found in 1962.

In 2002 after these two Hong Kong assignments of 13 and 19 years each, I felt I still had the energy left for a totally new kind of Maryknoll assignment, this time a "turn" back to the United States. When I heard that the coordination team of the Maryknoll Affiliates was searching for a priest member, I quickly volunteered, said my Hong Kong goodbyes and returned to take another "turn" directly in Society service. I joined former Maryknoll Lay Missioner Fred Goddard and Maryknoll Sister Janet Srebalus for a most rewarding six years of direct contact with Maryknoll Affiliates throughout the United States and in some of the mission regions. Fred and Janet were my special companions, and I discovered many more companions among the Affiliates. This was the first time in my Maryknoll life that I had ministered directly with committed Catholic women and men in the United States. As a coordination team, Fred, Janet, and I worked under the direction of and collaboration with Affiliate board members.

When my services were no longer needed on the Affiliate Coordinating Team I made what might prove to be my last "turn" in my Maryknoll Society journey and joined the Society Retirement Community in 2010. Membership in this Community has made it possible for me to continue to be available for occasional retreat and renewal work with both the Maryknoll Lay Missioners, and Maryknoll Affiliates. I was asked to be part of the Society Alumni Coordinating Committee (SACC) and have been able to reconnect with many former seminarians and former members of the Society. Society alumni are now understood to include all who were gifted with education in a Maryknoll Society seminary, present and former members combined. As a member of the Retirement Community, I have also been able to continue residence in the Washington, D.C., area where I am able to collaborate with the Maryknoll Office for Global Concerns as an associate focusing on Israeli and Palestinian issues. I represent this Office and Maryknoll on the board of Churches for Middle East Peace, and have contact with many other D.C.–based peace organizations and communities. I have spent most of my mission life traveling to and working in many places around the globe. In Washington, D.C., I continue to be involved globally.

And now, in 2011, during these last years of my journey, as I look back from where I have come as a priest member of the Maryknoll Society, what do I see ahead, for what do I hope as I try to see the road into the future? Much of my passage through the past 62 years reflects the passage of the Maryknoll Society. We are now celebrating our centennial as a Society; the Maryknoll Sisters will celebrate their centennial in 2012. During these two years we will all celebrate our centennial as a Maryknoll Movement of Maryknoll Sisters, Lay Missioners, Affiliates, and the wider Maryknoll Family. The next steps of the journey will of course be time limited for me, and all of us. As a Society we now see some 400 or so members with a median age of 78; we acknowledge quietly that just about half of these priest and Brother members are formally or informally retired. We wonder what Maryknoll as a Society and Maryknoll Movement will look like in the coming years.

The following words are obviously a projection into the future based on my personal Maryknoll journey with its many "turns" and generous companions along the way. These "turns" and companions were always surprises and proved to be the God-given gifts that have kept me walking the Maryknoll road as a priest missioner. There are many possible "turns" ahead for Maryknoll and the Church; I will try to name a few of them that seem to be already visible. What do I see and hope for the Maryknoll Society, the Maryknoll Movement, and the Church? What possible turns in the road seem to be emerging for these three components of my life up to the present; what dreams do I have for them?

A first possible turn: The Maryknoll Society will continue to decrease in size and in its role in the leadership of the Maryknoll Movement. At present it is primarily a clerical society within an increasingly "restorationist" institutional Church led by many Vatican and diocesan officials who seem to be trying to restore and grow the male, clerical, patriarchal, pre–Vatican II Church. During the Society Centennial celebrations there will be a forum to which all Society members will be invited, along with representatives of the other expressions of the Maryknoll Charism. Together they will look at possibilities and challenges for our future as a Society and as a Movement.

A dream: The Maryknoll Movement will see new life as the Society, Congregation, Association, and Affiliates move into a federation with shared leadership, mission education, fund raising and allocation, and mission service in churches of the world. The lay members of the Maryknoll Family will not only continue to provide financial support and the men and women to serve in the four present expressions of Maryknoll, but will share in the leadership of the Movement itself. Transparency, accountability, consensus, collaboration, and subsidiarity will be the defining qualities of these leaders.

Another turn: The majority of the "People of God Church" will continue to grow despite minimal support from the present forms of Church institutional leadership. It will develop and support leaders of living faith and proven competence. It will promote the priestly ministry of all the baptized, women and men, married and single; it will give little encouragement and support to the present forms of exclusively male, celibate priesthood, including that of the present clerical Maryknoll Society.

Another dream: The secular imperial, feudal model of hierarchical leadership will continue to implode and be replaced by more democratic modes of leadership relying more on competence and creativity and less on loyalty to centralized control. A process for a total revision of the rules and regulations guiding all the People of God (Canon Law) will begin at a third, truly ecumenical Vatican

Council of women and men leaders of the Catholic Church, lay, religious and clerical, along with representatives of other Christian denominations. This revision will be based on the Gospels rather than Imperial Roman secular law. It will be written in the light of the lived 2,000–year experience of faithful men and women based on the Mission of Jesus to proclaim and live the "Upside down Kingdom of God," free of all domination, where the first will be last.

A final turn: Women will share equally in the leadership of the Maryknoll Movement and the Church. Women and men will be our leaders, teachers, and Eucharistic ministers. They will not be a class apart but of and within the Movement and People of God; chosen by them to serve for periods of time limited only by their competence, willingness, and energy.

A final dream: Based on the lived experience of faithful, committed friendship over the past Gospel-infused 2,000 years, human sexuality and incarnational love will be fully recognized as God's special gifts to the human race, rather than as obstacles to be minimized or overcome. Celibacy will be respected as a gift to be personally received rather than an obligation for ministerial leadership. The People of God will give witness to our exploitive world of loving, equal, inclusive, mutually respectful relationships within and without marriage without patriarchal domination and sexual exploitation. The People of God will help all our brothers and sisters love and respect each other in and through their bodies; will teach each other ways to love and respect each other in body, mind, and spirit, rather than focus on promotion of guilt and regret for experiences of sexual domination and exploitation. Our understanding of the "deep" Incarnation will finally include the bodies of women, the earth, the cosmos, and all of creation.

❏

Jack lives in the Washington, D.C., area. As a member of the Maryknoll Retirement Community, he continues to work with Maryknoll Lay Missioners and Maryknoll Affiliates. He serves on the Society Alumni Coordinating Committee and collaborates with the Maryknoll Office for Global Concerns as an associate focusing on Israeli and Palestinian issues.

Always Connected

Hank Gromada ('67)

A FEW YEARS AGO, in the context of a group meeting, we were asked to do an exercise in which we had to write our autobiography in six words. Mine was as follows: *I am always connected to everyone.* When I have reflected back to the time 56 years ago when I decided to enter Maryknoll at the Venard, with a sense of wonder and with a spirit of searching. I have mused about what motivated me, back then and at that young age, to make that choice. This autobiographical statement (above) has provided the answer.

By reading the *Maryknoll* magazine *(The Field Afar)*, I came to a realization (naïve and not fully formed, at the time) that *I am always connected to everyone.* And, the response to that realization was, for me, inescapable; I knew I had to respond. The 5.5 years that I then spent in Maryknoll (at the Venard and at Glen Ellyn) during my formative years opened my mind and heart to that larger and universal reality. The whole issue of celibacy was not "on my radar screen" when I entered; and, when I left the seminary, I had come to the realization that I could live out this motivation in other ways and in other settings.

In brief, I have worked professionally as a school psychologist for 46 years. I have been married for almost 48 years; my wife Ruth and I have four adult sons and four granddaughters. My career had been focused on working with children and adolescents with serious emotional and social adjustment problems. During that time I had the opportunity to design and become the director of a residential and day treatment center and later to oversee programs and services for this population. Currently I continue to work on a half-time basis.

There is no doubt in my mind the there is a strong connection between the *calling* I had to join Maryknoll and my life's work, professionally, in my community, and in my family. Truly, *"I am always connected to everyone."*

❑

Hank and his wife, Ruth, live in Mitchellville, Maryland.

Our Lady of Maryknoll

Maryknoll Reflections

Jim MacDonald ('68)

YEARS BEFORE I ENTERED MARYKNOLL, I was being prepared for a Maryknoll-like experience. In the 1960s, the Catholic Church had a Peace Corp–like program that sent college graduates to Latin America. Having much more than my share of naïveté, while at a Catholic university in South Bend, Ind., I remember distinctly my worry that all the problems of South America would be solved before I graduated. There were plenty of problems remaining at graduation, but I only got as far south as a little mission school in Texas. While at a *cursillo* in Texas, I ran into the fiery Blase Bonpane, who had found himself an easy recruit, because I was ready.

The powers that be at Maryknoll decided that college graduates such as Biff Jenney, John Lieb, and yours truly, along with a dozen others, needed 26 credit hours of Latin to prepare us for speaking Chinese or Swahili, so we joined the class of '68 at Glen Ellen. Bill Houston. who attended the same college in South Bend, and was assigned to be my handler for my entry into seminary life. Bill had to remind me about 50 times in the first week that there was no talking on the stairs or in the bedrooms in preparation for working in the noise-filled cities of Asia and South America.

The next year was novitiate at Bedford, which I remember fondly, despite the German perfectionist who ran the place. As in the days of old, age had its privileges, such as driving the truck into town or to the dump with another old guy, Nim Horning. Most of my formation at Bedford happened outside of the classroom or spiritual exercises. Rooming with a classmate with my same last name, Bernie MacDonald, was a learning experience. He filled me

45

in on much of the history of the clan and the crazy Scots in general. We all had lots of fun with shifting schedules when Monday became Friday and Thursday's schedule was on Tuesday, except for the third week of the month. Captain Ray Finney refurbished the old whaling boat and set sail on the Concord River. Luckily, Ray and his crew were able to fight the current and were not swept out to sea. We were the class that moved from Bedford to Hingham. The brand new Hingham seemed a little sterile coming from our homey barn and stables in Bedford. Hingham, which was built in anticipation of increased vocations, seemed like a mistake to us, as we lost 30 percent of our classmates in that year.

I then went to the Knoll, where again classroom learning ranks very low in my memories. As Nim and I always said, we joined up to be priests, not theologians. One memory was a disappointment that I was not selected to go to Harlem for a summer. But Claude Harris, Al Stumph, and I won second prize and went to inner-city Ossining for an exciting summer. Fr. Fedders was slowly opening up the seminary and each class was permitted to own an auto—only for apostolic purposes of course. Al, Claude, and I became Maryknoll entrepreneurs buying a car and renting it out to classmates. I remember well a Maryknoll tradition that our class changed. At the beginning of first theology, I had been with the class for two years, while most of my classmates had been in the class for four to eight years. But I was the oldest, which anointed me "class senior," or head of the class for calling meetings and communicating with the faculty. It was the sixties and we did live in a democratic country, so we were able to convince the faculty that an elected leader was in order. We then elected one of the youngest, Andy Eichmann, to be our leader.

In those years, Maryknoll was opening itself to new types of formation for seminarians. As a result Marty Lowery, Al Stumph, and I completed a summer of Clinical Pastoral Training just before our final year. It was very helpful in the initial phase of learning some counseling skills. As I recall, there was a program at the Knoll the following year that helped us continue that type of learning.

Many of the memories are bits and pieces—of the building, of my room with the wonderful view, of Fr. Joe Grassi living next door, and, among the students, of serving in the priests' dining room, of shoe-leather liver and lamb with a strange green jelly. There was the "Christ figure" fad, during which everyone was seeing the Christ figure in all kinds of literature and movies, including James Bond flicks.

There was lots of talk of Small Christian Communities (SCC) that were making waves in Latin America. Steve Wood, Bill Houston, I, and a few others received permission to try living a little more communally, so we moved to the tower for a year. The experience was great and it also built up our leg muscles with all those steps. Just before ordination, my SCC friends were also very helpful in sending out a second set of letters to all my family, friends, and acquaintances telling them to ignore the first invitation or announcement because I would not be going on to ordination.

Do I have regrets? You bet, I missed the boat ride to Latin America with Grace Lines. I also missed learning Spanish at Maryknoll's great language school in Cochabamba [now called the Maryknoll Mission Center]. I missed the companionship of classmates and Maryknoll's focused sense of purpose. I missed the freedom of being taken care of—three squares a day and a place to sleep and play. But life moved on, and I used my accounting degree from Notre Dame to find a job in NYC, so I could continue to

Maryknoll Mission Center, Cochabamba, Bolivia

eat. John Fattor found us an inexpensive hole in the wall, which we fixed up so that we had a place to sleep.

While I didn't travel to faraway places, some of the beauty of Latin America did come to me when Irene Mora of Barranquilla, Colombia, said yes to my proposal of marriage. Most of the immigration red tape was made easy, because the U.S. counsel in Barranquilla, a Notre Dame graduate, was a guest at our wedding. We had fun living in the Big Apple for a year, but soon moved to the D.C. area and found a job with the training section of the Labor Department. Raising two kids in the new town, Columbia, Md., was a gratifying work of love. To say the least, we have learned a multitude of things from Anastasia, an environmentalist, and John Michael, an actor.

The echoes of Maryknoll were in my ears when our parish decided to partner with a parish in wartorn El Salvador. I was in the first delegation to visit that country and worked hard to convince my fellow parishioners to experience mission in this concrete way. In more recent years, I joined the first delegation to establish a partnership with a parish in Jamaica. I also participate in a monthly Maryknoll luncheon in D.C., where the Maryknoll spirit burns brightly as we keep up to date on classmates and former teachers, while at the same time solving the world's problems.

❏

Jim and Irene MacDonald are both retired in Columbia, Md. Their daughter, Anastasia, is an environmental entrepreneur and their son, John Michael, is an actor/director in nearby Washington, D.C. Irene, a "master gardner," spends many volunteer hours educating adults and children in gardening practices that preserve local streams and the Chesapeake Bay. Jim is a volunteer counselor in the SHIP program that assists people with complicated decisions involved in their participation in Medicare. His other fun activity is volunteering in the Head Start preschool program. Jim has also been a member of the Society Alumni Coordinating Committee, which meets at Maryknoll twice a year.

Ugali

Bill Murphy ('71)

Ugali –
   Immaculately swept dirt,
an African hut/home
   aroma of hay dripping
from recently rained upon
   thatched roof.

Ugali –
   – only the right hand.
A steaming mound of
   lovingly, laughingly
prepared corn meal
   In the dark
field coarsened hands of
   a dusky Sukuma woman.

Ugali –
   scratchy, firm
hot ball rolled
   in the right hand
A concave cup of
   corn swiped in spicy
stewed sauce.

Ugali –
   grainy and coarse
bland yet spiked.

A mushy meal
made meaningful
    by careful preparation
and conversation.

Ugali
    – a simple warm
welcome.

❏

Bill Murphy was born in San Francisco in 1944 and entered the Maryknoll Junior Seminary at Mt. View in 1958. He was ordained in 1971 and went to Tanzania, East Africa. Bill married his wife, Jane Zampitella, in 1983 and both are happily involved in a variety of educational and community-building activities. Ugali, the subject of his poem, was the staple food of the Sukuma tribe. It was the equivalent of potatoes for the Irish or polenta for the Italians. But as is evident from the poem, it was much more than mere food.

Faith of a Mustard Seed

Frank Luciani ('74)

MARYKNOLL INSPIRED ME to help those less fortunate. After I left the Novitiate in 1970 I began to work for the State of Pennsylvania in social services. I retired in 2007 after I had worked as a youth development counselor, Children Youth and Families (CYF) licensing representative, CYF regional supervisor, and a vocational rehabilitation counselor. In the midst of state employment I felt the need to help my parish revamp its Religious Education Program. I obtained my Masters in Religious Education and did just that. I helped revitalize everything from child formation, sacramental preparation, youth groups, RCIA, Scripture study, parish small group formation, and more.

In 1990 I became involved in St. Michael parish's social concerns committee. In prayer it came to me that as a parish we could help *some* needy people, but if we could get the other churches in town to join us we could make a much bigger impact. Some people told me it couldn't be done. Taking it to prayer again it came to me that if I had but the faith of a mustard seed I could move a mountain, that nothing was impossible with God. So I set out to do it. First I got five Protestant churches in town to join in on the idea. Their ministers wrote a letter to all the rest of the churches in town inviting them to a meeting to discuss the issue. Eleven churches sent representatives to our first meeting. They all liked the idea and they commissioned me to do research to help develop policies and procedures to develop an organization. In 1991 thirteen churches in town established the Good Shepherd Center and elected me as its first board president. Since that time the center has helped thousands of people with food, clothing, medical care, dental care, shelter, and appropriate referrals to other social service agencies. Today over twenty churches, literally every church in the Greenville area belongs. As a result there is not one needy person in a hundred square mile area that any church is aware of that doesn't get help. You can move a mountain with God's help. I have never lost the high ideals given to me at Maryknoll.

❑

Frank Luciani was born in 1947, the first born of eight children. He attended St. Michael School in Greenville, Pa., for 12 years and graduated from high school in 1965. He obtained a BA in Philosophy from Maryknoll College in 1969. He worked for the State of Pennsylvania for 30+ years in various social service positions before his retirement in 2007. He volunteered as a religious ed coordinator and received an MRE (Masters in Religious Education) from Gannon University in Erie, Pa. He married his first wife, Lia Azzato, in 1985. They had two girls, Gina, now 24, and Teresa, now 22. Lia died of ovarian cancer in 1998. He married his current wife, Tia Tofani, in 2007.

Chapel, Maryknoll College, Glen Ellyn, Illinois

Maryknoll and Me:
Part of the Story

Tom Quigley ('57)

IT WAS 1944. The war was winding down. I was one of only two freshmen to make the De Sales High School JV basketball team, and a priest friend gave me a pamphlet titled "You Too Can Be a Maryknoll Missioner." Written by Al Nevins, it sold for 10 cents and had a coupon to send in for more information. The 12 pages were filled with pictures of good-looking all-American types (including "former quarterback at Holy Cross, Father John Donovan"), guys in cassocks or playing hockey or blessing their mothers on ordination day or standing on the bridge of a ship, in clericals and fedoras, "on their way to their posts in South America." I sent it in, and a year later I was at the junior seminary in Buffalo, living at the Maryknoll house with a half dozen or so other guys interested in exploring this very popular, very American group called Maryknoll.

Throughout my freshman year I had begun thinking about the priesthood. I had gotten to know good priests at my parish, and Korea missioner Felix White, a local boy who had been interned by the Japanese and repatriated on the *Gripsholm*, was then at the Buffalo house. He'd been in a serious auto accident that smashed a leg and left him incapable of returning to the missions. He clearly was cultivating me. Although I found my freshman Latin a breeze, Felix noted that the quality of Latin instruction at my local high would not be adequate for seminary life, so why not look into studies at the Buffalo minor sem? I went up for a couple days, liked what I saw, and signed up.

A solid Latin grounding, of course, was the sine qua non for ordination in those days—or so we were told. I had marvelous teachers at St. Joseph's minor sem, did great in Latin (I still love the *Aeneid*), okay in Greek, and sailed through the rest of the (then standard) high school curriculum. As far as I can recall, only Denny Kraus from the Buffalo house joined me at Lakewood in the fall of 1948.

It was a good year. I enjoyed the scrub pine–filled campus of the old Newman School that counted F. Scott Fitzgerald among its alumni and was delighted with the strange accents of so many guys from Bahston and N'Yawk and Joisey. When, at the end of the year, half our class was to open up the brand new sem at Glen Ellyn, all of us from the western United States were Chicago-bound. Bill Kruegler from Troy, N.Y., was, like me, from Geneva, N.Y., a newly minted Westerner, so top-heavy was Maryknoll's intake from the coastal northeast. Guys from the east side of the Hudson, like Eddie Killackey from Yonkers, were still Easterners.

Before heading out to the Midwest, Al Zurowski and I had spent a lot of manual labor hours pulling down pine trees and talking about Europe, so we decided we'd hop a tramp steamer that summer and just go. He'd been in the Battle of the Bulge and was keen to revisit where he'd been shot at; I was just keen to see the museums, cathedrals and the wonders of the old world. We traveled third class from Naples to Southampton, staying at the Maryknoll House in Rome where a young Scripture scholar, Joe Grassi, was studying. A great trip, though Al and I never spoke again. Traveling takes its toll.

The three years at G.E. sped by quickly. The trips to Chicago opened up vistas of the then burgeoning lay apostolate—a few of us (including my buddy Al Schwartz) spent time with Red Sullivan of YCW, visited often with Pat and Patty Crowley of CFM, St. Benet bookshop, Friendship House, and more. A trip to Mundelein convinced us that Chicago priests must all be wussies, given the luxurious quarters and hired help that kept their seminarians from the joys of daily manual labor.

Art Kiernan was, of course, founding rector, and a stern taskmaster he was. ACK, or Ack-Ack as he was variously called, took his oversight duties seriously. Every Sunday afternoon we gathered in the chapel for his weekly "fireside chat," in which he outlined the many shortcomings of this impious rabble. At one of these he said he would see Brother Quigley in his office immediately after dinner. I could think of no outstanding breach of the Rule that I had committed, so it was with considerable surprise that he took out an envelope, addressed to me, and informed me that my disgraceful behavior during the previous summer spent at Lakewood would now prevent me from attending my brother's wedding the following April in New York.

All incoming mail was subject to being, as the rubber stamp proclaimed, "opened by the rector." Usually it was lavender paper, sometimes scented, with distinctly feminine handwriting that merited his prying. This envelope merely contained a photo of me and Larry Carroll, taken by this Indochinese gentleman who had been staying there during the summer. On the back, he wrote: In remembrance of your stay in Lakewood during the summer of 1951. *s/Ngo Dinh Diem*. The disgrace was that Diem, future president of Vietnam, had caught me practically *in flagrante*—there I was in cassock, opened at the neck, no collar and, by far worst of all, no cincture. Was this a portent of how I would observe celibacy? The story has a more or less happy ending. When I informed my mother, she thought it a very stupid thing and so told a friend of hers whose brother was married to a Benziger in New York who had adopted a child from Spellman's Foundling Home and—well, Ack soon heard that the cardinal archbishop of New York would be pleased if I were able to get to the wedding.

Even before that I had almost been expelled when, returning from summer vacation after sophomore year, I was found to have had what was then called a brush cut, which Father Rector took to be a sign of insubordination. He had warned us against developing what he called the Joe College look, clearly inappropriate for a future *alter Christus*.

After graduation, we went to Bedford for novitiate, a time of intense spiritual reflection. I recall just four things from those first four months. First, my buddy Bill Coll (not a "particular" friend—most of us didn't know why there was such concern about particular friendships), whose two older brothers were in the Jesuits, had to return to Pittsburgh when his mother died. Second, another buddy Al Schwartz, who found Maryknoll and most of the church in the United States altogether too bourgeois, decided to join Fr.

Lebbe's Société des Auxiliares des Missions. (SAMist Fr. Raymond de Jaeger had come to Glen Ellyn and had spoken of their principle of incardinating in the dioceses to which they were missioned. His cause is now moving forward, as is that of another but younger G.E. friend, Vince Capodanno.) Third, one night we were all woken by a great clanging of bells or something; it was a practical, electrical joke rigged up by a classmate who would make a lot more noise and cause headaches for Maryknoll later in Guatemala, Tom Melville. Fourth and finally, after ample reflection and good guidance from my spiritual director, I left Maryknoll and enrolled in Fordham's graduate school the following January.

Many of these "alumni" stories are beautiful accounts of how the experience of Maryknoll, ordained or not, led to great accomplishments or, at least, fully lived lives in service of others. My comfort zone is other. My style is different. But I do say that it was the time spent in Maryknoll, and my contact with dozens of Maryknollers over the years in Latin America and Asia, that has made my many years as foreign policy advisor for the U.S. bishops so thoroughly satisfying and rewarding. Thanks, James Anthony. Thanks Tarheel Apostle Tom Price. Thanks Maryknoll.

❑

In 1962, after finishing doctoral studies at Michigan on the GI Bill and a teaching fellowship, my wife, Catherine, and I moved with our three Ann Arbor–born babies to Washington, D.C., to head up the Council of International Lay Associations (CILA), housed in the Mission Secretariat offices of Fred McGuire, C.M. The following year, I was asked to take over the NCWC Foreign Visitors Office where, to the dismay of some bishops, I was active in opposing the Vietnam War. I then joined the Latin America Bureau under Mike Colonnese, John Considine's successor, and when that was phased out, joined Bryan Hehir's Justice and Peace office as advisor on Latin America. I retired in 2007 to supervise the education of our seven fabulous grandchildren.

How I Came to Maryknoll, Learned from Maryknoll, Left Maryknoll, and What Happened Afterwards

Nick Petraglia ('60)

I WAS A CHEMISTRY SENIOR at Queens College of City University of New York. I chose a chemistry major because I wanted to become a teacher or a doctor so that I could thereby help the needy. Then I had a sort of revelation. The most needy are in the developing countries and missioners specifically work for those people. So I therefore applied to Maryknoll and was sent to the Venard, the minor seminary (as a "delayed vocation") after attaining my bachelor's degree. I had to start there because of never having attended Catholic school and thereby never studying Latin. Then to attain the requisite philosophy I had to take two years of college at Glen Ellen. But finally I was with my class, the class of 1960. By the way, for whatever it's worth, the teaching at Maryknoll was not good! The rationale for persisting in that mediocrity must have been the belief that God would give these blessed men the grace of endurance? I was glad to hear that our Maryknoll students now go to more academic schools than our seminaries were. Then we went to the novitiate to pray and think hard about our vocation.

I realized that I was not that religious. I was a humanitarian, but did I feel that strongly about religion? Did I feel that I should commit myself first and foremost to the propagation of my religion? And then secondarily do works of charity? I wish it had not been all or nothing. I think I might have tried the Maryknoll missionary life if I could have had the option to opt out after a period of service. The number of dropouts before and after ordination suggests something in that vein as a good innovation. Present practice of exposure to missionary life before ordination and the success of our Maryknoll lay missioners, who commit to a term of several years, suggests the value of those formats.

Now I was a layman again! So I went into teaching without thinking too much about this as a crossroad in my life! What a chance this would have been to try something different like writing, i.e., journalism, which I enjoyed as a student. But instead I started teaching in junior high and "worked my way up" to SUNY (State University of New York) community colleges as I earned a master's degree and certification. Then I completed almost fifty years in a classroom. One of my best years was as a Fulbright teacher in Turkey, experiencing a different culture and the chance to travel. But, you know, I never felt completely happy as a teacher. Maybe I should have become a Jesuit where you can have a blend of the intellectual and active life?

Then I married. Wasn't it the thing to do then at that time in my life? Even though I never learned how to pick out the best woman to be my wife, I guess I'm fortunate that it turned out all right. I can imagine many guys out of the seminary marrying for the sake of getting married! Not knowing how to tell when and if you love someone enough to marry her and how to please and be pleased in the state of matrimony.

So here I am at 80+ years. Did my experience as a Maryknoller help me? Yes, I believe it did. I learned to appreciate the value of my religion—its discipline and universal morality. Unfortunately I did not learn to try other paths than the missionary priesthood or teaching as the opportunities arose to seek increased personal satisfaction and happiness.

As I approach the end of my life, I am appreciative of my experiences and learnings. How lucky I have been to be an American with so much opportunity. Thank you, Lord, and forgive me for not using my opportunities, my graces, as well as I should have.

❏

Nick Petraglia lives in Goshen, N.Y.

Some Grateful Thoughts

Andy Eichmann ('68)

THE 100TH ANNIVERSARY of the founding of the Maryknoll Society is being commemorated in many different ways. And isn't that about right? Maryknoll can be thought about and looked at from so many angles and aspects, it seems to me, because Maryknoll has always been about the people of Maryknoll, *Maryknollers*. And the prevailing tenor and atmosphere always seemed to me to be the recognition that each person has so many gifts and such uniqueness that should be fostered and nurtured. Each of us was encouraged in so many ways to experience his own value and try new things; and to come to realize, to support, and to prize in others *their* uniqueness and worth.

As I look back at my own experience from the vantage point of so many years I see that so many Maryknollers influenced me for my good in ways that were not always clear to me at the time. To mention but one group and indeed just a few of that group: the Maryknollers who were involved in helping me grow during my years in the seminary. I think of some wonderful things I was taught (but not always caught by me) in high school at the Venard, for example. The love of learning and treasuring another language, from George Ratermann (I never had a better teacher.); the love of reading and the enjoyment it can bring, from Thomas Tennissen; the strength and high expectations and humor that Dick Allen stood for; at Glen Ellyn the chance to learn from and work for Gene Kennedy (the special dignity and richness of the person); the wonderful and incredibly well-prepared classes in art Larry O'Neill provided that I still think of (you don't have to be a snob to enjoy art); the scholarly excellence and academic mastery of John

McConnell; the patience and warmth of a spiritual director like Tom Malone. Then there was the love for theology exhibited so strongly by Bill Frazier; the athletic endeavors led by Greg and Jack Keegan.; the openness and sheer charity of George Putnam; in the novitiate the brilliance and breadth of John McCormack. In the major seminary the kindness and push for excellence that I felt from Bill McCarthy; the forward thinking of Ed Malone in putting the seminary on the accredited academic map, so to speak; and the wondrous generosity in time and expertise of Art Brown in the library with the soundness and balance of Bill Heffernan.

Just some thoughts about how fortunate and truly blessed I feel to have been around such people—Maryknollers all. Not to mention all the Maryknollers and former Maryknollers whom I was privileged to be with as schoolmates and colleagues after ordination. People who were there for me in so many ways and in so many times.

To all of you, my heartfelt thanks.

❏

Debbie and Andy are enjoying life in the glories of Colorado. They spend lots of time outdoors hiking and skiing and also share in some volunteering. Their three sons have all married within the last two years and so now they are delighted to have three daughters too. Their kids live in Colorado, Boston, and San Diego, so they've got things covered.

A Maryknoll Story

Bill Allen ('57)

THE UNENLIGHTENED SAY I AM OLD NOW, but I may be good for a story anyway. Upon retirement in June 1994 from Federal Parole in New York City, I told all those obviously edgy individuals who had backed me in tough and funny times that I had had the honor of living and working with two great groups of out-side-the-box men and women for long periods of time, namely, them and, also, the men and women of Maryknoll. Both had provided me with ideals; both had shown me the best and worst examples of attempting to be faithful to those ideals. It was the truth of their struggles and my own that initiated the long molding of maturity into my life and, for that, I owe too much to repay.

At the Venard, I almost lost my mental balance trying to be holy like a fellow student who had a prayer book packed with cards and prayers that he had to say every day or be damned. I was caught up in his dementia until I heard that he had been sent home. It was there also an Old China Hand miraculously taught us four years of classical Latin in five months.

Philosophy at the Knoll really provided me with a sense of Society and of being a seminarian simply by living at the Knoll with the major administrators and seeing so many black cassocks walking through the halls and sitting in the refectory. However, a fluid caste system existed in that the Chosen, the subdeacons and deacons, apparently had no wish to associate with lowly philosophers. I did not think negatively about them, though, since I thoroughly believed that they were fully engaged in holy things, yet unknown to me, and that hierarchy had been divinely instituted for the good of nonhierarchy beings.

Theology was different with apologetics, dogmatic theology, Scripture, canon law, church history, and a very brief Hebrew try-out. Serious matters with some strange teachers. The texts were in Latin, but, fortunately for all, Latin was no longer the language of the classroom. This positive contrasted negatively with the intrusion of the "Roman Index of Forbidden Books" on our reading and teachers' presentations. That single mandate effectively dumbed down whatever we studied. It was hard to adjust to the idea that every story only had one side. It's justification fully hinged on a benign and divine hierarchy's goodwill in protecting the flock. Still, what lifted our spirits were the thousand facets of intelligence, rashness, moderation, affability, seriousness, and jokes of the students. That environment was so positive that it created its own validity and sureness in my mind. Like the Church imperfect, the Maryknoll imperfect and its continuance served as my guide to the future.

After ordination in 1957, responsibility indicated two different

Maryknoll in Bolivia

62

areas of Bolivia. Fifteen years later, how I defined responsibility had changed significantly. My original messianism in what and how to proceed had morphed into a conciliar mode without absolute presumptions and communicated in fluent language. These concepts developed through years of cooperating with the Aymara people and Maryknoll priests, Sisters, and Brothers and other Sister's groups with whom I shared happy and beautiful years of companionship, study, and a waking, hard-won maturity.

I give thanks now to all these men and women, living and deceased, within the Society and without. I honor them for their ascendant trying. I still count on them and am blessed to be considered one with them on our continuing uneasy pilgrimage.

Aim for perfection…and the God of love and peace will be with you. 2 Cor 13.

❑

In 1973, Bill returned from Bolivia to NYC , earned a master's in bilingual /urban education and briefly taught at a Brooklyn public school. He obtained employment with Federal Parole/Probation, married his wife, Eduarda, whom he had known in Bolivia as a coworker "Laura" Sister in the Aymara highlands. They have three children, two girls, and a boy, who now has two young sons. Upon Federal retirement, Bill obtained a further Masters in ESL and has been teaching immigrants at a nearby community college since. Edu and he are in the *Interchange* book, and invite readers to come for a swim and a beer during the hot summer. They returned to Rockaway Beach, a long-blessed strip of sand, a long time ago and live a hop, a skip, and a jump from the unbelievable ocean.

Maryknoll's Micaiah

Jim Collignon ('53)

The king said, "How often must I put you on oath to tell me nothing but the truth in the name of Yahweh?" Then Micaiah spoke: "I have seen all Israel scattered on the mountains like sheep without a shepherd." And Yahweh said, "These have no master, let each go home unmolested." At this point the king of Israel said to Jehoshaphat, "Did I not tell you that he never gives me favorable prophecies, but only unfavorable ones?" – 1 Kings 22: 16–18

DURING THE UPCOMING ANNIVERSARY CELEBRATION we are going to hear a lot of cheery things about the next century of mission work to be done by Maryknollers. It's not going to happen. We are in the end-time of our Society and this is a dangerous time. In my last sermon in the seminary chapel I compared the Society to Enron. The worse things got at Enron, the worse they continued to get. Along with the cheery, optimistic setting of goals and the like, we need a provisional plan that will manage or control the continuing decline of the Society. BP now knows something about planning only for success and not for failure—provisional only. I don't know what the future will bring—provisional and precautionary. Something that began in the Spirit must not end in the flesh.

In Vatican II we were encouraged to read the signs of the times. Now Rome will do that for us. What are the signs in our society that might guide our Society as we approach the anniversary year?

Let us consider first our Society, then our society.

We began as a clerical Society. That kind of Society has no future except in monastic settings and with the new ultraconservative groups. We began as a national mission society similar to European models. That kind of Society also is finished.

This winding down we are experiencing is not a problem peculiar to Maryknoll. All the national mission societies are encountering the same problem. We are all part of the same phenomenon—a response to the call to preach the gospel. But this response was conditioned by the imperial intentions of the various sending nations. We were part of that movement. And as that movement comes to an end so does our mission. For some years when I was in Taiwan I taught English. I was interested in introducing Blake and Frost and other worthies to my students. My students were interested in participating in the American economy. And I knew it.

Our society has changed in a great variety of ways. The sexual revolution, which touched our seminary in the early sixties, now touches all of our young people at even earlier ages with raw and romantic depictions of sex. I remember when my little sisters would censor *Life* magazine so that an older brother would not meet temptation. No longer. Nowadays applicants to enter a seminary have sexual histories as often as not, and these have to be looked into.

Moreover, mandatory celibacy has given us a feeling of superiority over other Christian bodies that is not helpful to ecumenical endeavors. It is a pillar of clericalism. It must go. Believers and nonbelievers alike recognize this.

It seems the Catholic faithful are doing quite well without the guidance of their clergy: frequent confession or even occasional confession has been dropped, along with novenas, Friday abstinence, most devotions, indulgences, and of course, the ban on contraception, and all without a word from us. Clericalism has had its day, and it could be that even the more conservative among us would agree that this is a good development. What kind of society would Maryknoll be without its clerical foundation?

There will be mission in the future if the Church is healthy, and it will be realized in forms and structures now unknown to us. It will be done by churches like our own, but let us hope that this new effort will not be competitive. All the denominations had to be represented in Taiwan, each with its own name. In Taiwan a commonly asked question is, "Are you Catholic or are you a Christian?" We are speaking of a Church response to the requirements of the gospel, not the evangelizing activity of contending churches. The ecumenical movement affects most of us. The world reality is not at all what it was when we entered the Society and neither is the Church reality, and I think most of us would agree that that's the way it should be. Time marches on.

Our position with regard to the American church has changed greatly. Most promoters—and we had a great band of promoters in the Fifties and Sixties—could feel that we were the darlings of our church. That hasn't been true for several decades. In my experience the younger clergy simply aren't interested in us. Their conservative bent is one reason for this. Though presently we are a very conservative Society, we are often still perceived as Marxist. I wonder if our developers these days meet many bishops who are enthusiastic about us, and perhaps for the same reason. I remember asking a Newark pastor for a magazine date and he said, "I wouldn't foist that rag on my people." (He turned out to be a rather pleasant fellow, but no date.) Pastors will still give us a date when they want a Sunday off, but things are different nowadays and I think most developers would agree. Everything is different: a Society no longer capable of doing real missionary work in the way we defined it years ago (establishing the Church), the American church, and the world.

I say the world because it is growing increasingly secular. This is one of the signs of the times. To witness against this trend is all well and good, but meanwhile we are negatively affected by it. Some see signs of promise in this situation, that a different and better way of being church will evolve. But meanwhile the Society will continue to decline. I don't see it prospering in this new situation.

Finally, today there is a great difference in the way Catholics regard the missionary enterprise. I am sure that many, the better educated many perhaps, feel that we foreign priests should not try to convert people who are satisfied with their religious beliefs and who practice a religion that has more good qualities than we formerly were able to discern. We joined Maryknoll at a time when mission was supported by a majority of the Catholic faithful. We went off to the seminary when most of our friends and relatives thought we were, to a degree, heroic. My dentist replaced all my fillings with gold at no cost to me because he believed that in China nothing of this kind could be done for me. Support like this was very important to us, especially in the difficult times, whether in the seminary or on the missions. Well, that kind of support is no longer there. "Why convert them—they're happy?"

Most of us grew up in a ghetto church. We were all for the missions, Catholic missions not Protestant missions. We had nuns teaching us in those days and often they were keen about the missions. They encouraged us to make little donations. I remember when we could give a name to a Chinese orphan if we made a certain contribution. The ghetto no longer binds us. The nuns are gone. And it is likely that in this secular age teenagers will stop going to church for a time. Talk about change!

In what ways must Maryknoll change? An anomaly we must face is the disproportion between the Society's rather puny mission effort now being made and the overhead costs of maintaining this effort. The salaries of our various staffs at the Knoll, their retirement benefits and their health plans, all owed them in justice —the disproportion is staggering. It is a good thing the faithful in the pews are not aware of this—or is it? Much of the money that goes to the missions goes to support staff. Self-support, if it ever really was a goal, has not been achieved. We have to take care of our elderly, but let's not call it mission.

One solution to the problem of great expenditures is to sell our assets. The Society has sold many properties in this country for a great deal of money. So far as I know, the sale prices of these properties have not often been made known to the membership. So much for transparency.

But I would like to speak of one property in particular, the center house in Taichung. We bought this property in the early Fifties for peanuts. Today it is worth many millions of U.S. dollars. Since a house of that size and a property of that size are no longer needed by the Society, it makes a lot of sense to practical people to sell it. However, the Society and the diocese have been at loggerheads for decades over who really owns the property. The matter has even been taken to Rome. While a case can be made that we own it, there is a problem: the Taichung Diocese has a need and use for this fine urban property. What their need and use might be is for the local church to decide. And while we Maryknollers might not know what the value of this property is, the local people have a pretty good idea. For us to sell it and walk off with the bundle would be scandalous to the local Catholics and would undo some of the work we tried to do there. Talk about mission! And even if the resident Maryknollers there were to approve of such a sale and anticipate moving to new lodgings to be built, the scandal would be the same. And would it be good for Maryknoll to have all that money to spend? Money corrupts. Consider Wall Street. The Society is entering a hazardous, dangerous time.

What about the Knoll itself? To paraphrase Yeats, "Things fall apart; the Center cannot hold." How should we dispose of that property if the decline continues? Or should we? Or if we do, do we need the supervision of the bishops? I don't know the answers to these questions but they should be asked. We never really owned the property after all. The American church leased it to us and it remains theirs.

I believe it was James A. who used to say, "God doesn't need Maryknoll." We could repeat these words, quite confident that in actuality He really did. James A. was right again.

We joined a movement whose time had come. We worked with our fellows during our Society's peak years. We all experienced its decline along with our own physical decline. We are grateful to God that we were chosen to be part of it, whether for a short time or over the long run. Kingdoms rise and fall. The American Church is undergoing an extreme makeover these days. We are part of that.

❏

Jim Collignon was born in St. Cloud, Minn. in 1926, entered The Venard in 1944 and was ordained in 1953. After teaching music in Glen Ellyn for two years, he was assigned to Taiwan. All together he served there for 25 years. After nine years on promotion he was assigned to Kenya since he was persona non grata in Taiwan. But after three years there bad health forced him to return to the States. Over the years he has helped out in various American parishes. A few years ago he married and left the Society. His health is pretty good, all things considered, and he is enjoying life in Louisville.

Invitations and Camaraderie

Jack Clancey ('68)

DURING A MISSIOLOGY CLASS a couple of months before our class was ordained, Bob Ledogar suggested that we should be ready to discern the needs of the local communities where we would be living to see how best we could serve the people. I recall that he illustrated his advice by saying some might assist people by driving a tractor and working as a tractor mechanic. I have never found myself in a situation requiring the skills of a tractor driver or mechanic, but I adopted the principle.

Although possessing a fertile imagination, I never could have foreseen the paths I have traveled as a result of adopting that simple principle. After language school, while serving in a parish, I accepted the invitation to assist several groups of Young Christian Workers, most of whom had started working in factories at about age 11 and were then working long hours, seven days a week. I met regularly with them in the evenings and during their lunch breaks and tried to help them develop a sense of dignity and self-respect, as well as basic leadership skills.

The next invitation came from our bishop, who invited me to join a team of university chaplains. Some years later, after attending a number of Asia-level meetings, I was invited to be the university student chaplain, first for East Asia and then all of Asia, which brought me to many parts of Asia. I helped to develop training programs that started with a three- to four-day "exposure experience" of living with poor families (slum dwellers, farmers, minority groups, etc.), followed by two weeks of input from social scientists and then input from Scripture scholars and theologians, culminating in the students discussing ways they, as students and then as young graduates, could respond to the needs of the poor.

On one occasion, when I approached a bishop for a letter of support to be sent to funding agencies for some programs we were planning, I was invited to become executive secretary for the Office of Student Chaplains and Non-Formal Education of the Federation of Asian Bishops' Conferences. At a time when everyone, perhaps particularly some bishops, appeared to be frightened of radical students, I always arranged for some students to share their perspectives at the start of the meetings I had with the bishops and always invited bishops to attend the training programs we held for students and chaplains.

The next step in my journey was back to the world of workers, this time on an Asian level, when I worked at the Asian Center for the Progress of Peoples. The goal of the project was to raise awareness of workers' problems and struggles for justice and to develop support for unions. The work included documentation, meetings, advocacy, and various means to try to get church groups to offer support to workers and unions. I again traveled around Asia, as well as to Australia, the United States, and Europe.

At one stage I was invited to teach a course on Marxism for the philosophy section of the local seminary and then was invited to give the same course to the Maryknoll Sisters, who invited Sisters from many other communities to attend.

At age 50, after someone advised me to study law, I found myself attending night school. Three years later I obtained a law degree from the University of London. One academic year later I had a postgraduate certificate in law from the University of Hong Kong and after working two years as a trainee, I was registered as a solicitor of the High Court of the Hong Kong Special Administrative Region (SAR) of the People's Republic of China.

In between all of the above, in response to various invitations, I worked with some young university graduates to establish a night school for workers and agreed to help some young doctors by serving for ten years as the chair of the Hong Kong Workers Health Center—I'm currently assisting as a legal adviser—helped establish a small publication house, and was persuaded by César Chávez to be the chair of his Hong Kong "No Grapes Campaign." How could I resist the invitation from a Maryknoll Sister to be a member of the board of Our Lady of Maryknoll Hospital?

Since 1997 I have been serving as the chair of the Asian Human Rights Commission. I am a founding executive committee member of a democracy advocacy group: Power for Democracy, as well as the China Human Rights Lawyers Concern Group. As part of the movement for democracy in Hong Kong, I was requested to be a candidate from the legal constituency for the 800-person election committee that selected the chief executive of the Hong Kong SAR. Out of 42 candidates I came in ninth and am now a member of that committee. According to my classmate Dick Madsen this has made me a member of the local power elite, but I hasten to add, if that is so, I am on the far fringes. My wife Edith was selected for one of the slots allocated to the Catholic Church and as a result we are the only couple on the committee.

There is a Chinese curse: "May you live in interesting times!" To the contrary, I have found these times to be a blessing and as a result I can relate thousands of interesting anecdotes, which I have begun sharing with my children and to whom I have promised I would someday write them all down.

Over the decades I have experienced the solidarity of the Maryknoll Community. The relationships developed during our seminary years have led to long-term friendships that are rekindled through correspondence and on those occasions when our paths cross. I have always benefited from the support of superiors, as well as other Maryknollers, even though I was seldom involved in "traditional" work. Although I found myself in places very few, if any, Maryknollers reached, such as Cape Comorin at the southern tip of India, or the forests in the Western Ghats Mountains between Kerala and Tamil Nadu, or Burma (1979), or Saigon (February 1975), when I visited areas where Maryknollers live and work, from the beautiful regional house in Tokyo to a semi-shack in Bangladesh, I always enjoyed their generous hospitality. I traveled to a number of countries with Msgr. George Higgins—who was a good friend and strong supporter of Maryknoll—to meet with his labor contacts and mine, after which we "exchanged analysis." I have also been inspired by the creative work of some Maryknollers. One example: I published a Chinese version of the Orbis book, *The Radical Bible*, after Ed Gerlock showed me the Filipino language version he had produced. Mine made it to the presses first because of martial law in the Philippines. I "found" a Korean Minjung

Theology book and negotiated to have it copublished with Orbis. From time to time I would submit photos and articles to *Maryknoll* magazine. During one period of time I accepted the invitation to work with the Maryknoll Justice and Peace Committee. Most recently, in response to a request from Tom Peyton, I have organized a small group of lawyers, working pro bono, to take up the case of a murderer who is seeking a determinate sentence.

I also have the distinction of being the father of two Maryknollers, as both my daughters graduated from Maryknoll Convent School in Hong Kong.

When I first arrived in Hong Kong in 1968, I was given a space in the attic of the Stanley House to put my trunks. I saw painted on the rafters the names of all the regions in China where Maryknollers had worked. My trunks were placed not far from some that had been there for decades. I sensed the aura of being not far from those who had made their unique contributions to working for the Kingdom of God and serving people in China and realized I was about to become part of a history. In recent years I have heard favorable comments about some of the contributions I have made for justice and human rights. I hope that my contributions have enhanced, and will continue to enhance, the reputation of Maryknoll.

On this anniversary I wish to express my gratitude to Maryknoll and Maryknollers for the camaraderie I have enjoyed, being a member of a community that has provided service to, and fought for justice for, the least of our brothers and sisters in many parts of the world.

❏

Since marrying in 1985, Jack and Edith have continued to live in Hong Kong. In order to provide better care for the children, Edith transitioned from being a social worker to a mother/housewife in 1997. She still takes up some part-time teaching jobs and has been active with various voluntary works. They are blessed with two daughters and one son: Josephine (23), Bridget (20), and John (18). Josephine is an occupational therapist in a major government hospital, currently specializing in both hand therapy and work-related cases. Bridget will soon obtain her associate degree in English and plans to continue university studies. John is currently studying at the Hong Kong Design Institute and would like to specialize in architectural design.

Maryknoll's Impact:
The First 100 Years

Donald Howard ('69)

I WAS A PART OF MARYKNOLL FOR NINE YEARS, but Maryknoll has been a significant and integral part of my whole life. Maryknoll was in its 45th year when I entered the Venard in Clarks Summit, Pa., in 1956. I was 14, still in my formative years, young, not yet an adult, but I had a very positive experience academically, socially, and spiritually. My values, my beliefs, and my character were shaped by the people who are "Maryknoll."

The priests, Brothers, and students at the Venard, at Glen Ellyn, and at Hingham impressed me with their focus and dedication to Maryknoll's mission. Their warmth, friendliness, humor, and dedication were genuine and supportive. We studied, worked, and prayed together, and we grew and developed intellectually, spiritually and socially together. We were a family.

When I was at Glen Ellyn, in my junior and senior years, I was assigned to work on a special project with Father Thomas Malone, a former missioner in China and the former rector of Maryknoll Seminary in Ossining, N.Y. Father Malone wanted me to help him initiate and write a necrology to highlight the lives and accomplishments of deceased Maryknoll missioners. I was to research and write a brief biography for each priest, like an obituary.

Father Malone intended that a copy of the necrology, arranged by the date of death, would be in the sacristy of every Maryknoll church or chapel in the world, so when the priests were about to offer Mass they could see which deceased Maryknoller they would pray for that day.

There was a format to which we had to strictly adhere. Each person was to have one page. Their photograph was at the top. Their name, dates of birth, ordination, and death were under the photo. The text was to be the same length for each priest. It included where they were from, which mission region(s) they were assigned to, and what significant issues they faced, as well as their successful accomplishments.

At first, I found this project difficult in terms of the depth of research required. Also, the task of writing was a bit daunting. However, as each obituary was completed, I felt I knew these men very well. I had a unique perspective. I was astounded by the variety and the volume of the kind of work these great missioners had completed. They each have made the world a better place by their work and dedication.

Maryknoll will continue to inspire me in the next hundred years.

❑

Donald Howard was born in New York City in 1942. He attended the Venard, Glen Ellyn and the Hingham Novitiate (1956–1965). He married Virginia Whelan of NYC in 1969. They have three children and five grandchildren. He received his master's in education from Manhattan College (1970). At Fordham University, he earned both a PhD in curriculum and instruction (1972) and an EdD in educational administration and supervision (1981). He has taught at both high school and college levels and has been a principal and superintendent of schools in New York State for more than 40 years. He retired from public service in 2004 and is now principal of a Catholic school in the Diocese of Bridgeport, Conn.

What Being a Missionary Meant to Me, or... My Life in the Philippines

Robert Nugent

JUNE 11, 1966—33 of us are ordained as priests for Maryknoll. A whirlwind two days of activities culminates the following day with the departure ceremony. Several weeks later 12, or was it 13, of us meet up again in San Francisco to be shipped to the Orient by boat. The numbers 12 or 13 may or may not be significant unless you equate the biblical 12 or the unlucky 13. But we were going to four countries: South Korea, Japan, Taiwan, and the Philippines. And we were going in different old Liberty ships.

Sometime around August 1, after two departure cancellations, from the Oakland docks, the three of us going to the Philippines—Frank Paris, Denny Mahon, and myself—were able to embark and sail...at least for a mile. The ship developed a problem near Alcatraz Island and began to run in circles. We desperately wanted to see ourselves sail under the Golden Gate Bridge and wave bye-bye to the sending country. Never happened. We fell asleep and when we awoke we were on the high, misty Pacific Ocean never to see land again for 17 days.

What land! As we neared Japan a typhoon was developing. I must interject here that the Liberty ship we were on was bound for Saigon via Pusan and Manila. Its cargo was mostly war materials for Vietnam. The deck was loaded with U.S. Air Force trucks. Only God knew what was below deck and God wasn't talking. We three were the only passengers; three messengers of peace riding on top of war materials heading to the Orient. Followers of St. Paul, meditate on that while I get back to the typhoon. The typhoon was bearing down on us so instead of going south of Japan and into Pusan, we cut through the middle of Japan via the Inland Sea. The typhoon caught us. The boat rocked up and down. I strapped myself into bed, said good-bye to Mother Earth, saw nine years of training for two months of priesthood, hoped Maryknoll would give us a great write-up in the magazine, and fell asleep. Woke up in the calm waters of Pusan Harbor, the sun was full in all its glory. Maryknoll—hold that martyr article. Three days later we were in rainy, flood-ravaged Manila. Thank God I went to Glen Ellyn, where they forced us out to play basketball or whatever—handball, you say—in wind, rain, and snow. My companions and I were ready to begin our missionary careers.

We spent a year in language school then went out to our parishes. Maryknoll had been assigned a huge area. The Society took it over in 1958 with four parishes and by the time it was "turned over" to the Filipino Church in the mid 1980s it had grown to at least 22 parishes. On and on the statistics grew, but statistics are not the point of this little essay.

The first thing I had to do as a new missionary was to forget about the Catholic Church—USA style. The Father, Son, and Holy Spirit had already been to the Philippines. My job was to find Them—in myself and in the people. The veteran Maryknollers showed me the way. There were the credit unions, the farm programs, the *cursillos*, the list was long. You got down and dirty with the folks. You were to be present with them in their joys, hopes, and sorrows. Wherever they were you had to be. There were also churches to be built, schools, rectories. Some of our Maryknollers actually lived in boarded up shacks with *nipa* or GI sheet roofs. We were subject to frequent floods, dirt roads that were sometimes impossible to pass. I don't think any of us stopped to count the physical, mental, or other hardships. We were, so to speak, actually following the road of St. Paul, and probably did not give it much thought. After language school I spent the next two years working as a priest associate, as is now called, in two parishes and then moved to the seat of our growing prelature, Tagum. I found myself working in the junior seminary, teaching in the local high school and college, and eventually becoming the youth director of our Social Action Center. I watched my elder Maryknoll companions and learned from them; I watched and mixed with the people and learned from them. It was the beginning of a growing period of unrest for the Church and the people of the Philippines. It was pre–martial law. People were stirring, becoming agitated, wanting change. The youth, with whom I became greatly involved with, were caught between whether they should follow the Church in creating change or joining the forces in the mountains for a faster way of change. This was the real life of a missionary. Being in the middle with his/her people.

After several months' furlough and updating at home, I went back to the Philippines in 1971 and began a four-year service as parish priest of our very rural parish of Gov. Generoso, popularly known as Sigaboy. This was to be my first assignment out on the plank on my own, no Maryknoller around to help. Eventually Maryknoll sent me another Knoller to ease my burden. I was following the founding pastor of this parish, Mike Hiegel. He was a legend. A Mother Teresa figure to parishioners and even to some of us Maryknollers. As a 19-year-old he was in the Normandy invasion. He died at Maryknoll early in 1978 at the age of 52 from illness, his life spent and exhausted in the service to others. After I left the parish in 1975 the parishioners erected a statue of him. OK, Mike, exit stage right—this is *my* story.

Sigaboy I must tell you is on the world map. It is a finger-long peninsula on the southeast corner of Mindanao, the southernmost island of the Philippines. The parish of Sigaboy was on the left and the parish of Mati on the right. Sigaboy was the name of the village where the dirt road ended and we had to cover the remaining 20 miles south by using an outrigger motor boat to visit our numerous barrios. The reason for this long geographical description will become evident in a moment.

Our key work in the diocese and in Sigaboy at that time was building small Christian communities. Educating each barrio to become self-sustaining, self-governing, and self-supporting and able to run on its own, even to the point of conducting weekly church services on its own. There is a whole story around that program. It was not limited to the training of church leaders only, but community leaders. It was also the time when the idea of lay missionaries began to develop. I was hooked from the beginning and it became the focus of my remaining years in the Philippines, which you will see.

September 21, 1972—Martial law is declared in the Philippines. Many parishes including our own have some parish staff and members of our parish arrested. The Maryknoll radio station in Tagum is closed. Things are bad, but not terribly bad. Sigaboy is far from Manila. We weather through. Most people eventually get released. They had done nothing subversive. The whole story is too large to tell here. But there is a biggie. There are parts of the Bible that take on a whole new meaning in these situations. Bible discussions take on a lived dimension. No longer do you read about the New Testament. You read about us living in the here and now.

December 3, 1974—Feast of St. Francis Xavier, fiesta day in Sigaboy. Near nightfall I learn that a small group of rebels has holed up in one of our barrios and that some members of a group of Filipino national guard–type troops sent to contain them did not return to the *población*. Next day, Filipino army troops come into the *población*, some are on their way to the area of disturbance. We are in virtual lockdown—difficult to get in or out of town.

December 8—Take our outrigger canoe and head down to say Mass on a mountaintop barrio near the area of conflict. The quietness of the Mass competes with the sound of gunfire coming from government airplanes attacking the rebel position. Is this what the missionary goes through? Was there a class at Ossining on this and I missed it?

Sometime in mid December—Army HQ in Mati asks Jack Walsh, Mati parish priest, to contact me to go down to the conflict area using our parish boat to pick up the government troop dead. We all meet in the Sigaboy convento. The army gives us body bags. Takes Jack and me an hour to convince my boat driver to drive us. Unknown to the Army his sister and brother are already in the hills in another part of the province fighting on the rebel side against these same army troops. We finally go down. Our group consists of four: Jack, the boat driver, myself, and one of my catechists. The catechist will know some of the dead; he grew up from childhood with them. We bring back nine bodies/ parts thereof. I cannot eat for 24 hours. Dry heaves. Five days later I screw up enough courage to go down to the barrio next to the area of dispute.

Find out the rebels were watching us pick up the bodies. I was known to the barrio residents. Jack and I were dressed in white cassocks (when we started to approach the area of the bodies). We ditched the cassocks. The heat and the tension were killing us. The rebels let us do our thing. On this near-Christmas visit I said Mass for these people. They were still alive to celebrate Christmas. Is this the work of a missionary? I shall carry the events of December 1974 with me to the grave.

I go home to Boston for much of 1975. Take summer updating courses at Boston College followed by the fall renewal program at Maryknoll, N.Y.

Return to the Philippines in January 1976 to begin to live in a barrio in the diocese of Butuan with a team of several lay people. This is one of the first steps in a process that will lead to Maryknoll beginning a Filipino Lay Missionary program. We live in a wooden house with a *nipa* roof and bamboo slat flooring. The potty is a lean-to behind the house. We pray together, farm together, minister to the surrounding barrios. We get flooded out, have snakes for visitors. I have to take off in October to have hernia surgery in Davao; the lay folks continue to run on without me. The program does work.

In March 1977 the regional council names me to start the Filipino Lay Missionary program. I organize, recruit, train, and send out the first groups of lay missionaries. All kinds of people pitch in and help. The area church is no longer the receiving church, it is the sending church. In reality, we all become part of a sharing church. The word missionary takes on added meaning. The program that we began evolves into the Philippine Catholic Lay Mission under total control of the Filipino Church sending lay missionaries not only within the Philippines but also to surrounding countries. It still lives on today.

I have another epiphany moment. I have reached a point in my life where if I am to continue my life in the Philippines, I must more deeply enter into an understanding of the spirituality of the Filipino people. And my own as well.

I leave the Lay Program in 1979 and come home to the States for furlough. I return to the Philippines later that year and am invited into the prelature of Iligan. I go with the intention of living alone in a barrio and studying how the faith of the Filipino influences his/her daily life. I want to answer the question of my epiphany moment mentioned above. The bishop—he has a bigger request. He wants me to do my thing and also he wants a history written of the prelature of Iligan. The church in this area goes back to the time of the arrival of the Spanish missionaries in the 1600s. The bishop sets me up in an abandoned seminary with unused classrooms for meetings—even comes with a kitchen setup—and he hires the back-up staff. And the building is surrounded with tall grasses containing snakes, again. What am I doing here? I have no formal academic training in history. I have no formal training in research. But I have discovered that I have a gift for gathering people who have these credentials and much more—the people who will bene-fit from the gifts these creatures from hallowed halls have to present. With guidance from all these people—big and small—we embark on our mission. The project culminates three years later in the publication of two volumes: *An Historical Profile of the Prela-ture of Iligan* and *Final Report of the Pastoral Research Project.*

Along the way on this three-year journey we climbed many mountains. Mountains of which some I wish I and others never had to climb. The area in which the studies are conducted is the heart of the Muslim–Christian conflict. This has been going on for nearly a century and at the time of our project it was in full bloom. One Sunday night in my so-called hidden seminary I heard a series of booms. It was a hand grenade attack in the main square. An attack by some group on motorcycles on the folks getting out of the after-noon Mass. The report said about 20 were killed and over 100 wounded. Another Sunday, morning this time, we are conducting the pastoral research interviews in a mountain barrio. Suddenly people are streaming down the hillside from a neighboring barrio. It is under siege. People see me. I am known in the area. People stop running. I must look like Jesus. No way the bad guys are going to continue pursuit when there is an American priest in the barrio who might get hurt and bring a lot more attention on their bad be-havior than they had planned. Sometime later I am taking a rest in one of the neighboring town rectories. The parish priest is away. Some folks come and get me. There has been an ambush in an area nearby. There are casualties. They want me to give the last rites. OK, I'm the missionary. Don't need any theological tome for this one. Just be with the people. Presence. Pray with them.

There is an American Columban staying in the bishop's house during this period. He is one of the consultors for the research project and comes from Rhode Island, a neighboring state of my home base, Massachusetts. About five years older than me. He served in Vietnam as a chaplain with another priest from Boston who is a lifetime friend of mine. Both were wounded. The Columban and I shared much on being a priest in the middle of atrocities. He is experienced. He asked to be in the middle of such trouble, I never did. I got there by accident. We share often. He has a metal plate in his head. Pain is a constant. He is a missionary.

What did it mean to be a missionary? I really can't tell you, I am still working it out. Outside of the Sigaboy uprising, on which I had to make a report to the Maryknoll Philippine Regional Council, this is the first time I have ever put my thoughts on paper. I have talked it over with other priests and ministry people. Then we go off and share a snack together. My wife and I don't discuss it much. She was the leader of our basic research team and lived in Iligan. Her father, a medical doctor, was killed by Muslims in the middle of a Christian–Muslim conflict. The Muslims, who considered him their doctor, although he was Christian, found him trying to heal Christian and Muslim victims of the conflict. Other members of her family have been kidnapped over the years. Some experiences are hard to discuss.

This paper was hard to write. In the end I turn to St. Paul and his words on going out to people and the many physical and mental costs involved.

In early 1983 I looked in the gas tank; the meter was on empty. Seventeen years was all I could give. I headed home to the States. The Spirit was calling me to something new. I had to take the time to find out what. Walk another plank.

❏

Bob and Pinky Nugent, 13627 W Countryside Dr., Sun City West, AZ 85375. Email: bobpink@att.net.

A Priest Forever

Joe Bukovchik ('66)

MY MOM WAS FROM SLOVAKIA and my dad was first gen-eration American. The idea of the priesthood came from them who thought that was the highest calling and so I wanted that. I became an altar boy in the third grade and served Mass through high school and into seminary days.

I was born in Stratford, Conn., on March 22, 1939, and baptized at Holy Name of Jesus Church on April 9, 1939. At my baptism, Fr. Grinvalski prophesied to my parents as he held me, "This boy will become a priest!"

I grew up with two older sisters, Marian and Frances, and a younger brother, Raymond. My mom, Julia, was a professional up-holstery sewer, housewife, gardener, canner, and head of our household. My dad, Stephen, was an upholsterer who later in life worked at Sikorsky Aircraft. I realized that I had one of the best, loving, faith-filled moms in all the world. Dad died in 1985 at 82 and Mom died in 2003 at 95.

In September 1953, I entered the Venard, Maryknoll's junior seminary, in Clark's Summit, Pa. as a high school freshman, where I remained until February 2, 1954. I returned home because I was homesick and only 13 years old at the time. After high school, I re-entered Maryknoll, went back to the Venard for four months, and then in January 1958, transferred to Glen Ellyn. I graduated from there in June 1961, and then was at the Bedford Novitiate for a year until 1962. I was ordained on June 11, 1966, at Maryknoll and assigned to Japan.

In August 1966, I set sail for Japan, a 13-day cruise to Yokohama Bay from the Oakland Army Pier. The evening before disembarking from Isthmian Lines' USS *Steel Flyer*, I gathered my fellow Maryknoll priests on deck as we were bathed in the amber lights of the ship. The shore lights of Japan twinkled in the distance. Then I raised my hands high toward Japan and said, "Paul had his missionary journeys, and this is my first missionary journey. Oh, Japan, Japan, if only you knew what is in store for you!" If anyone were to have told me that evening that I would meet my wife in Japan, I would have said, "Wash your mouth out!"

Several weeks later, I began language studies at the Franciscan Language School, St. Joseph's Institute at Rapping, in Tokyo. All missionaries new to Japan spent their first two years there. Sr. Ann Boyce, from Bayside, Queens, N.Y., was already a second-year language student.

After my nine-year sexual hibernation in the seminary, I delighted to be around Sr. Ann and the other women studying there. Within two weeks, Ann and I felt so close that we celebrated our "spiritual marriage" by enjoying a meal in the revolving restaurant atop the Hotel New Otani in Tokyo. (This hotel was used as the building in the 007 movie "You Only Live Twice.") The Spirit worked quickly to bring us together. During my first year of language school, Ann and I were just great celibate friends. Then on July 26, 1967, Ann left for her mission in Okinawa. That was the day I realized that I was in love with her. I cried so hard at her absence and I saved a handkerchief filled with my tears to remember that dark day.

We began to write, call, send voice tapes back and forth, and our friendship deepened over 1,000 miles of water. Fortunately, distance is no barrier to love. In November 1967, I traveled to Toyota, Japan, home of the famous car manufacturer. It was there after celebrating the Eucharist that Fr. John Shields, M.M., asked me a life-changing question: "What is most important in life for you?"

After some thought, I answered, "To be a Maryknoll priest here in Japan." Then I asked him. He said, "To be a fully realized baptized Christian." That stunned me! I thought he would give the same answer that I gave. While I defined myself primarily in terms of the clerical system, he defined himself primarily within the personal lines of being a baptized follower of Christ. The two views are very different. I immediately said to him, "If I thought like that, I would have to get married!" He looked at me and said, "I too am planning to get married!"

After returning to Tokyo, I wondered how I could square my experience of loving Ann with being a priest. So I looked in the New Testament and saw that the first apostles were married. I thought, Jesus is the same yesterday, today, and tomorrow. What He did then, He does now; that is, He is still choosing married disciples. I then realized that no one can take away from me the freedom Jesus gives. I saw that the mandatory law of celibacy is a sinful structure at the heart of our church. Since Jesus chose married disciples then, they must still be good for Jesus now since Jesus is the same yesterday, today and tomorrow. I felt exhilarated by this personal discovery, but in 1967, that insight was not widely accepted. As I began the process of leaving Japan, I thought, Well, after I marry, I'll make a few new Christians. As it turned out, God made five wonderful Christian daughters through us, with eight living grandchildren and one in heaven along with a daughter we lost during Ann's second pregnancy.

When I left Maryknoll, Fr. John McCormack, the superior general told me, "Go and never come back." I understood his remark as a personal one, and not one made on behalf of the Maryknoll community. Several years later, Fr. John also married, as did my rector, Fr. George Weber, and most of my ordained classmates. I heard that only after he left Maryknoll did Fr. McCormack feel bad at the way he treated other priests who left the Society to marry.

When I visited the N.Y. Archdiocesan chancery office to apply for a dispensation from the obligation of celibacy, I was met by a solemn faced Msgr. Quinn. He told me that I would be granted a dispensation from celibacy, but only if I gave a solemn promise to never celebrate the sacraments peculiar to the priesthood. I looked at him and replied, "I will give you a solemn promise that I will celebrate the sacraments peculiar to the priesthood and that I will pray for you." He replied, "But how can you?"

I felt the Holy Spirit speak through me as I answered, "In elementary school, I learned that all the sacraments are acts of Christ. How can Christ fight against Christ in the sacramental system?

Marriage and priesthood are compatible." The monsignor thought hard, was stymied, and then said, "Ah, but we have a law." I should have answered, "And according to that law, I must die!"

I read Fr. Godfrey Diekman's two-volume work on the history of marriage and found that for most of the first millennia, Christian marriage took place according to the culture and local customs of the place, and such marriages were considered sacramental. Indeed, until the eighth century, only the upper clergy were allowed a church wedding. So Ann and I felt free to marry anywhere according to our more ancient Christian tradition. Ann and I were married at Staten Island City Hall on May 7, 1968. Our marriage was blessed in December 1978 at the Mission San Luis Rey in Oceanside, Calif., when our four daughters marched down the aisle with us in their red and white checked dresses Ann had made. When it came time to give Fr. Martin McKeon the wedding rings, our four-year-old, Juleann, at first didn't want them removed from the little pillow she carried. Ted Gresh, M.M., class of 1965, was our best man.

After leaving Maryknoll in March 1968, I earned an MSW in 1971 at Fordham University in NYC and worked as a social worker for 32 years, primarily in adoptions.

During the years we lived in New York, Ann and I were members of the Society of Priests for a Free Ministry (SPFM), the forerunner of the Corps of Resigned Priests United for Service (Corpus). When we moved to California in 1972, we tried to organize the married priests of the San Diego area, but were unsuccessful. At the time there were at least several hundreds of married priests here.

In July 1985, I read that there was going to be a universal synod of married Catholic priests in Rome in late August. It would be the first such meeting in Rome since the twelfth century! After a special Saturday evening Mass at St. Francis Catholic Church in Vista, Calif., I was able to make a simple announcement asking the parishioners to pray for the synod's success. As I was making this 30-second announcement, an inner voice said to me, "Direct your announcement to Dr. Jim Esch." Jim, a medical doctor, was sitting in the last pew. I kept on talking and ignored the voice. The voice spoke again, "No, say it to Jim!" So as I was closing my remarks, I looked at Jim and finished my remarks. As I was walking away from the lectern, Jim came hurrying up the aisle and asked, "How would you and Ann like to attend the synod in Rome?" I answered that we'd love to go, but we couldn't afford it. He asked me to get the particulars on the synod and let him know.

The synod was a month away, and a week later, Jim saw me and asked if I had gotten the particulars. I had made no attempt to do so, and he importuned me to get them. He told me to give them to a mutual friend who headed a small Christian group who in turn would give the details to him. He said, "On Sunday we'll have a picnic in the park. Give the information to John McDonnell." I finally got the particulars and gave them to John, not thinking much about it. It would cost $3,000 to attend. On the way home from the picnic, I was waiting for a red light to change and spoke with God saying, "Oh God, there are so many worthwhile causes to which money like that could be given. You couldn't be interested in a cause like this! There are so many others." And God said, "I am interested in everything."

I began to cry because at that instant, I knew then that Ann and I would be going to Rome in just 3 weeks! We would have to buy plane tickets, get passports, and arrange for babysitting. The entire experience went off smoothly.

The synod was to be held at an old Roman Catholic convento in Rome, but two weeks before the synod was to begin, the Vatican forbade the Sisters to lend us its use. What was to be done? When the generous Italian Communists heard about our plight, they opened their training school to us. There we held our international synod in Arricia, Italy, about 15 miles outside of Rome. I felt re-ordained by the Spirit as I attended the gathering. We were from countries in Africa, South America, and Europe, as well as from Canada, the United States, Newfoundland, and other places—all saying with one voice that marriage and priesthood are compatible. Soon thereafter, Corpus America was born.

Corpus caught on here in San Diego, and Ann and I were instrumental along with others in beginning the local chapter. In 1996, Ann chaired the group hosting the 1996 National Corpus Conference at UCSD, La Jolla.

Through the years, I have volunteered within the institutional church, but always felt the loss of the use of the priesthood to which I was called. Three times I was removed from ministry.

Once I officiated at a fellow priest's wedding in Los Angeles and when word instantly got back to San Diego, I was removed from parish service. Twice more similar things happened. I was finally removed by Bishop Brom of San Diego from teaching RCIA in 1993 for being a married priest—even though Bishop Brom's sister is married to a priest. Since then, I have shaken the institutional dust from my feet and finally got the Spirit's message to minister to the marginated. I continue to perform many marriage ceremonies.

I retired in October 2004, and regularly fly my 36-year-old, radio-controlled quarter-scale Piper Cub, quarter-scale Gypsy Moth, and quarter-scale Fokker D-VII. In November 2004, Ann and I took a cruise to the Caribbean, and in November 2005, we made a pilgrimage to the Holy Land for two weeks. We've traveled extensively and have a Hawaiian cruise planned for March 2011. Retirement is the best time Ann and I are having.

For 15 years, our small faith community of the Holy Spirit has met for the Eucharist and a potluck breakfast or dinner afterwards. We helped to support Neela Pieris in Sri Lanka, who headed an orphanage just east of Colombo, the capital. One hundred percent of every collection was given to Christ's poor. Though we were few, our collection averaged $1,000 a month. At the orphanage in Sri Lanka, where we sent most of our offerings, our donations went a long way to feeding Christ's orphans. It is amazing how the Spirit collects the funds!

Being a priest has been quite an experience. Why? Because I did not get the kind of priesthood I thought I was getting. Instead of receiving a priesthood that would primarily function within the confines of the institution of the Church, I received a priesthood that functions in God's greater world. Jesus is open to not just Christians, but to all. I wish to be like Him and so minister to anyone in need of priestly service.

❏

Joe and Ann Bukovchik live in Vista, Calif., where they continue their Christian ministries in their retirement.

What Does Maryknoll Mean to Me?

Steve Cuthbertson ('71)

What does Maryknoll mean to me?
What has Maryknoll done for me?
What has it meant for me to have been in
Maryknoll?
What does it feel like to have been "chosen"
—albeit for a brief 2.5 years?

I ALWAYS WANTED TO BE A MISSIONARY, even though I did not know what that really meant.

Being a part of the Maryknoll community taught me more about people and life than I could have ever imagined. I learned that the poor—poor people—are not to be feared, but rather to be loved and accepted as individuals, who through one misfortune or another are forced to survive in some of the most deplorable circumstances.

While conducting a census in a poor parish in Chicago, I met a single mother who was struggling to raise her three children in a slum. Her husband had died and left her to raise and nourish three children on her own. She was so gracious, when I knocked on her door. She offered me food—and she had so little to give. We talked and shared an hour that I shall never forget. She does not know how much her kindness meant to me. She was not to be feared. She was not someone to be hated nor was she someone to be pitied. She was doing the very best she could and making a life for her children—setting an example for all those she came into contact with.

She was not bitter. She was concerned for others—she was setting a positive example for her children and for me.

Then there was the luxury suite at Hingham, Mass. What an opportunity—everyone should be so fortunate and blessed. To have your own room, gym, handball courts, chef, and the choice of classes you take or create on your own. I was given a gift: a year to reflect on the past and plan for the future. I learned how to play the guitar and participated in liturgical celebrations as an active participant—no longer a passive observer. I had the opportunity to give my first, and only, homily.

I addressed our brothers on the meaning of Mary, our mother, and was able to thoughtfully address the significance of Mary and how she and my own mother shared so many things in common. I was not the easiest son to raise.

I still remember the Brother who cared for the "estate." Here was another example of an individual giving of himself unselfishly. He never knew how much his actions influenced me.

I taught high school boys CCD. What a challenge—it was not until I began visiting the students in their homes that I realized how important my teaching had become. When I honored one student's stated desire not to visit his home, I heard it from everyone. What he said was not what he meant. The home visit was arranged and I learned another life-long lesson—I can be most helpful at times by listening.

It was in Massachusetts that I met the Kelly family. Gerry Kelly was going to celebrate his first Mass in his hometown church, Saint Joseph's. He asked our musical group, if we would play a folk mass. His sisters Sheila and Kathy were in charge of making the arrangements. No big deal. We had played at numerous church services before. The Kelly's were a great family and even invited some of us to visit them at a cottage they rented at Hampton Beach. We had a great time, working on the music, sharing ideas, and getting to know one another. This proved to be far more significant than playing music for Fr. Gerry's first home Mass.

Then I made the trip to the Knoll. I was given only four months. In these months, I experienced things I hope never to repeat in my life. I never want to say to another person, "I cannot be the friend you want me to be." How horrible it was of me to be so selfish. How to do the opposite of listening. What had I learned over the last two years? Obviously, it was not enough. And then, quite un-expectedly, the table was reversed on me and I experienced what it felt like not to be a "best friend." Prior to Maryknoll, these two events would not have meant that much. However, the whole atmosphere among the seminarians at Maryknoll was that of caring for, supporting, and accepting one another. I was just beginning to understand and feel what it was like to be a servant with a mission.

My time at Maryknoll was up. The Lord had prepared me to leave and care for others.

The most important person in my life, I met while in Maryknoll: Kathy, the sister of Fr. Gerry Kelly. We eventually married and have three children, Kim, Andrea, and Sean. We were fortunate to have been married by Father Gerry and had some of the same Maryknollers play music at our Mass at St Joseph's. Gerry baptized and married all of our three children.

He and many Maryknoll priests and fellow seminarians are intricately involved in our lives to this day—from brother-in-law (Joe Sullivan), trusted financial advisor (Joe Graziano), skiing partner (Pat Murphy), and good friend (Bill Murphy). I am blessed to have an extended family that now includes a son-in-law from Iraq, a son-in-law who loves hockey, snowboarding, and the Broncos, and an Italian daughter-in-law, who teaches kindergarten. Kathy and I have seven grandchildren.

I cannot imagine a better life. Thanks to all Maryknoll priests, Brothers, Sisters, and lay missioners. Sharing life and the "missionary spirit" with you all has had a positive influence on my life and those I come into contact with day after day. One day at a time.

❑

Steve worked construction after leaving Maryknoll so he could travel to Africa and Europe. He then did social services work in Colorado, where he and Kathy married. They moved to Cleveland where he earned an MSW degree. Returning to Colorado he worked in both the public and private sectors. He is presently employed as a personal property appraiser for Summit County. He and Kathy have two daughters, a son, and seven grandchildren.

The Gift of Global Vision

Dan Driscoll-Shaw ('66)

IN GOD'S EYES the Pacific Ocean is no wider than the Ohio River. This global vision is the greatest gift I have received from Maryknoll.

It hit me early on. One night, when I was a seminarian at Glen Ellyn, we had a presentation on Guatemala. There in the front row, totally attentive, was Fr. Fred Dietz, a veteran China missioner. That he was so absorbed struck me deeply. Here was one of the "ol' China hands" totally engrossed, as if he might one day go to mission there himself. That touched my heart and sparked a vision that would be nurtured and strengthened by so many all my days in Maryknoll.

I am humbled to say that later, when I was serving in the barrios of Caracas, Venezuela, Fr. Dietz would send me a donation from time to time, as I know he did with other fellows. This just cemented that truly universal, catholic DNA of Maryknoll, which should be that of the entire Catholic Church.

It was so much a part of my faith that when I served in Venezuela and Nicaragua, we would take up a collection, certainly almost all coins, for the victims of natural disasters or violence in Bangladesh or Burundi or wherever, in order to share the Good News of our oneness with all our sisters and brothers around the world. The people would pick up on this global vision and offer spontaneous prayers for the victims of those tragedies.

Further, I have always been proud of *Maryknoll* magazine, *Revista,* and Orbis Books and their mission to share that global vision.

From there it was a natural step to the justice and peace commitment of my life both in the Society and after I moved on. To know that the passion of Christ was being repeated in the passion of the world called for solidarity and action, particularly where the U.S. government and multinational corporations were leaving their giant footprints.

I rejoice that now I am part of an interfaith pastoral team visiting immigrant detainees in our local county jail, who are from so many of the countries where Maryknollers have served. And in every Eucharist, when the presider prays, "Lord, remember your Church throughout the world," my heart burns with Maryknoll's global vision, and I so wish it were not such a big secret in our Church. ❑

Dan Driscoll-Shaw married his wife, Patty Shaw, in 1995. They live in Huntley, Ill., about 50 miles west of Chicago. He currently works full-time as a Spanish interpreter at a local hospital and is active in Maryknoll Affiliates.

The Joy of the Road

Fr. John K. Halbert, M.M. (1932–2008)

The joy of the missioner is the joy of the road...

The joy of the road:
in being sent to the world,
*   in being sent as Jesus was sent:*
*   to begin again Jesus' journey,*
Jesus who is the Way, the way to the Father
*   To our elusive God.*
The surprising joy of meeting God along the way.

The joy of the road:
*   in hearing God's voice in the strange tongues,*
*   of nameless people in foreign culture;*
*   to converse with the Samaritan woman*
*   who worships in spirit and in truth,*
*   to answer the plea of the Roman man*
*   whose child is sick and close to death.*
The surprising joy of life transformed where God speaks.

The joy of the road:
*   in traveling light, not encumbered by fishing nets*
*   and extra tunics in order to catch:*
*   blind Bartimaeus, who in seeing again,*
*   wishes to dance on the journey;*
*   loyal Philip who, though seeing,*

still confused the way;
The surprising joy of treasured companions
when baggage is left behind.

The joy of the road:
in the daily bread, the Broken Bread of Life,
enlivening the sharing of communion
to caring for the crowd;
becoming food for those in need.
The surprising joy of hosting God, so hungry and so poor.

The joy of the road:
in nowhere to lay one's head;
in the challenge of the storm to brave a sea so large
in a boat so small; in the peace of humble dwelling

to gather in His name.
The surprising joy of God's everywhere,
in turmoil and in peace.

The joy of the road:
in the inward journey: to the mountain of light,
to be transformed;
to the reality of darkness, to be transfixed.
The surprising joy of heaven now in the journey of the Way.

❏

John Kenneth Halbert was born February 29, 1932, in Drexel Hill, Pa. He attended Villanova College for one year, studying engineering, then entered Maryknoll in September 1951 at Lakewood, N.J., and was ordained on June 13, 1959. He filled numerous educational and administrative roles in the Society and served as a missioner in El Salvador from 1972 to 1978.

Acceptance of Challenging Life Events

LeRoy Spaniol ('66)

ACCEPTANCE IS ONE OF THE HARDER TASKS when adapting to challenging life events. Acceptance means seeing and acknowledging all the various aspects of our experience without judgment. Self-blame and negative judgments are barriers to acceptance. They can lead to disbelief or even denial because it is hard to accept what we devalue. Yet, acceptance does not mean approval, or even disapproval; nor does it mean being passive or giving up. Acceptance means seeing and acknowledging what is. Acceptance allows us to take the practical steps that help us to experience our life in a more grounded way.

Seeing and acknowledging "what is" seems like a simple task at first. Don't we do this all the time? Unfortunately, even an introductory exposure to psychology shows us that this is not so easy. We have a tendency to "color" our perceptions with our past learnings, or to project feelings and meanings onto what we perceive. For example, if our past learnings have taught us to devalue ourselves, then we may automatically find current experiences to validate that judgment. Not surprisingly, certain meditative and focusing approaches require a lengthy practice in "seeing what is" because our personal history has often distorted our perceptions. We can learn to be sensitive to our vulnerabilities in perceiving. We can come to know ourselves well enough to recognize when we are most likely to override "what is" with our conditioned ideas, feelings, and sensations. We can learn how to be open to "what is" without being overwhelmed or intimidated by our history or our fears.

Acceptance is a journey and not an event. It is not simply a matter of making a decision, because it involves both our emotional and cognitive aspects. It requires resolving this decision emotionally and through our actions. Our emotions tend to lag behind our decisions. This is why emotional change can be so wrenching and painful. Action helps to deepen and work through our emotional commitment to our decision. We can develop confidence in our acceptance by facing the feelings that acceptance brings up in us and through the actions that concretize acceptance in our life.

"What" we accept includes both what we perceive as our strengths, as well as our deficits. We need to accept "all" of ourselves. Acceptance is difficult because it builds on hope. However, hope, when defined as improvement, may be beyond the scope of some of our experiences, especially those that involve death or terminal or degenerative disorders. So where does our hope come from in these instances? For some, faith gives us hope. For example, I believe that life is not all about me, but that I am here to enhance and celebrate life in general and the lives of people around me. I accept suffering as a part of my life, without having to understand it or explain it. I believe there is a larger meaning and purpose to my life. I believe that God is with me and will give me the strength to bear what life gives me. Spiritual reading helps me to have a broader perspective than myself and to see that I am connected to a larger whole.

What about people without faith? Where does their hope come from? Without the foundation of hope, acceptance can be too terrifying. The solution of some people is to look outside of themselves for the answer to their hopelessness. This is actually an important step in a shift in consciousness from the self to others. Remember, people are not only reeling from the trauma of their life, but also from the awesome self-absorption that can result from any traumatic situation, with its heightened sense of personal impact on the self and its needs and wants. The hopelessness people feel is for themselves! It is natural to become very self-centered. This is a very lonely, alienated, and painful place to be. To shift to a realization that life is not all about me, but that I am about life, is an important attitudinal shift that can actually give us back our life and give us some hope. But it requires a shift from a focus on our self, our own needs and wants, our own losses, to a focus on some-one or something outside of ourselves.

Acceptance also requires dealing with loss. This includes the loss of the person we were before the acceptance, the loss of our defenses that had kept us safe but perhaps unfulfilled, the loss of the dreams of what could have been, and the changes in our personal relationships. Facing these fears can be very painful. Dealing with loss is not an easy task. Yet acceptance means seeing ourselves as we are, without judging ourselves, our bottom line. We need to begin our new life from where we are.

Acceptance involves facing ourselves directly and fully. The task is to see ourselves for who we are and what we are, without judging ourselves. Our own internal barriers and external barriers protect us from seeing ourselves directly and fully. Internal barriers are often called defenses. Defenses are really a way of protecting ourselves from the eruption of feelings that would occur without their protection. Defenses are a way of keeping ourselves safe from a perceived threat. Over time these defensive reactions become habitual and autonomous. People in our environment learn to support our defenses because we teach them how to do it. This is not a conscious effort, but people often find a way to work together to support their mutual defenses. When we begin to see ourselves more directly and fully, we may initially feel more anxious and vulnerable. And people around us may feel the same way because the rules of the relationship are being changed. Knowing that our changed perceptions can cause discomfort can help us to deal with our own feelings, and can help us to build a new way of relating with people around us.

Acceptance involves forgiveness. In acceptance we forgive life for what life has given us to deal with. We don't blame life for being unfair. Life is not under our full control. Life happens, and we are often left to deal with something we would not have chosen.

Effective coping with what life has given us builds on acceptance. It builds on reality. As we feel more confidence in ourselves, we begin to acknowledge other aspects of ourselves that are also part of our reality. These include our many strengths, our inner wisdom, and our relationships with family and friends. We gradually begin to identify with these other aspects of ourselves and to realize that we can call upon them as needed.

Acceptance can lead to compassion—compassion for ourselves and compassion for others. With acceptance we become less judging of ourselves and others. We become more focused on what we require to have a life, and how to get those resources. We begin to be interested in how to help other people with their acceptance.

Acceptance may reduce unnecessary pain and anguish. We are able to stop struggling with what we don't want to see or acknowledge. Anguish is replaced with the ordinary suffering that comes with dealing directly with the often-uncomfortable realities of our life.

Acceptance is courageous. Courage can be defined as the ability to make a commitment to an imperfect process. This is what we do when we accept ourselves. Our acceptance comes from our hope. We begin to believe that hope is possible, even if it means seeing the glass as half-full rather than half-empty. As that hope takes root, we can make a commitment to ourselves and to our acceptance, and to do whatever is necessary to bring it about—knowing that it is not a perfect process. There are risks, there are dangers, there are failures, and there are successes in life. And this is OK. This is courageous.

❏

LeRoy Spaniol, PhD, attended the Venard and graduated from Maryknoll College in 1961. He received his doctorate from the University of Wisconsin in 1974 in rehabilitation counseling and taught at Boston University for 31 years. He is now retired. While at Maryknoll he enjoyed writing in a variety of formats and felt supported in his writing skills development. While at Boston University he founded and was executive publisher of a professional journal, authored 18 books, plus wrote many book chapters and numerous articles. He continues to enjoy writing and publishing in his retirement.

A Tremendous Liberation

John T. Moran ('70)

I HAD HAD LOTS OF FUN, LOTS OF LAUGHS in my college years. Though I wasn't a leader in our class at Maryknoll Glen Ellyn, still I had a nice bunch of friends. But all laughter and fun disappeared from my life in the summer after graduation in 1965.

My parents had come out to Chicago for my graduation with my little brother and my two sisters. It was the first time on a plane for all of them. With the exception of one trip by car and one by bus, I had gone back and forth between Chicago and New York by plane during my college years, but it still was a thrill to get on an airplane and fly. Back in the 1960s people actually got dressed up for a flight.

It was great to have my family there for graduation. Months later back at home, my mother asked me why I didn't say something about my decision to leave the seminary when they were out there for graduation. I'm not sure that I had begun to think about it then, or if instead, the issue began in earnest after they left and the festivities were over.

The next year in my seminary training for the Catholic missionary priesthood with Maryknoll was called novitiate. It struck fear into my heart to contemplate such large globs of time when I'd have nothing to do but think. There would be no classes, no homework, no study, no exams. It would be a "spiritual" year.

That summer spent in the seminary following graduation was a preview of the novitiate. We had no classes, but remained at the seminary until we were released to go home in August. There was lots of thinking along with a desire to get it all outside of me, even though that would mean confessing to another human being. I wanted to get up the courage to talk to a priest, but my first step was to muster the courage to discuss the matter with a friend. I managed to talk to Tom Murphy of Boston, and John Hamm of Staten Island, but the final and necessary step was to talk to a priest. But which one?

It didn't take me long to decide on Father Tom Malone, a white-haired old man with an extremely gentle voice and manner. Though old, he was in good shape, having been an avid athlete all his life.

I went to see him one evening in his room. I can't remember what I said or anything he said, except for my comment about the transom over his door. I noticed it was open. I was afraid someone would overhear the terrible thing I was saying. The only thing I know is that I told him that I felt I should leave the seminary. I don't remember anything of what he said, though I know he did nothing to dissuade me.

Out of courtesy, I told the priest on my unit, Father McGinn, that I was leaving Maryknoll and the reason why. He told me that he had known someone like me in the Society and that his life in the priesthood was unhappy.

I wrote a letter to my parents and told them I was coming home for good. Both my mother and my father wrote me letters support-ing my decision though I'm sure they would have liked to see me a priest, especially my mother. On a lighter note, I was surprised to learn when I got home that my mother had thrown my bed out. Now someone would have to sleep on the couch.

I set about finding a job, particularly a job teaching, to avoid be-ing drafted. It was 1965 and the war in Vietnam was heating up.

My first night home, or maybe a few nights later, my father asked me to go out with him to a bar. Years later, long after my fa-ther had died in 1975, my mother told me he did it with the intention of getting me drunk, so I'd tell them what was going on inside me. The bar was a dingy unappealing place, and I was not used to drinking. Ironic that I was so uncomfortable being in a bar drinking; years later I wound up spending much too much time in bars drinking much too much alcohol. Anyway, I asked my father if we could leave after one drink, or maybe it was two.

We walked around the neighborhood. I don't remember any-thing I said other than something about same-sex attraction, as

Maryknoll College, Glen Ellyn, Illinois

though being in the seminary was the problem; and I can't recall anything my father said, except that I hear my father gently responding to me that he wondered whether there were priests "that way." There was no criticism in his voice, whether of me or of the Church; he was a loving father, and a loyal and fervent Catholic, remaining so until the day he died.

The funny thing is he and I never spoke of it again. Memory of that conversation with my father only came back to me recently for no particular reason. I don't know what my father told my mother about our conversation that evening in the summer of 1965. Strangely, it didn't occur to me to ask her in the very difficult conversation we had in 1985 when I told her about my same-sex attraction.

My psychotherapist had recommended that I share with my mother this core part of my identity. He said a mother's love trumps any religion, except maybe the Mormon religion, and some other one I don't remember But I resisted telling her, fearing that it would upset her too much. Later on I changed my mind when I started seeing a man who I thought might become the life partner I'd been searching for in the ten years since I'd come out in 1975. That man and I didn't become partners, but more importantly, I was well on the road toward discarding the secretiveness about that part of my life. It was the beginning of a tremendous liberation.

Today, 40 years later, the Vatican denies the priesthood to gay men, even though they make the same promise to live chaste asexual lives in the same way heterosexual priests do. I smile to myself now when I think back to 1965 when I, like most of my generation, thought I was the only one. Society sent the strongest message that my condition was shameful, perverse, disgusting. For me it was society, not the Church, that made me suffer so much. I went to the Church and Christ for some comfort and peace. Many see the Church as their oppressor, not hard to understand when we are categorized as "disordered human beings with a special inclination to evil."

Yes, I smile now because I have survived. Western civilization is gradually shedding all the oppression of gay men and women. What a different world we inhabit today, 40 years after I left Maryknoll. A breath of fresh air from the modern world displaced some stale (some would say noxious) air in the Church, as was the aim of Pope John XXIII when he convened Vatican II in 1963.

Forty years in Biblical numerology means a long time. What can we expect 40 years from now? Imagine.

The above memoir was submitted in 2005 in a writing class at the college at 60, a program of the liberal arts department of Fordham University for retirees.

❑

John spent half his working life teaching, first at Rice High School, Harlem, then at Glen Cove High School on Long Island. In 1987, he left teaching to work as a lawyer for the New York City Department of Correction, having earned a JD at Fordham Law School. In the late 1980s through the 1990s, John devoted a lot of energy to the movement for gay rights in Queens, which led to visibility for gay women and men all across the borough along with a significant place at the table in Queens politics. John has been single most of his life, except for his domestic partnership with S.M. Kim, a Korean immigrant, which ended after 11 years when Kim returned to Korea. Since retiring in 2000, John has been enjoying life in New York City. Currently the major focus in his life is the care and support of his sister Mary Ann, who was left almost speechless by two strokes in 2007.

This Is Thy Aim,
Thy Sacred Call

Art Melville ('61)

I AM DEEPLY GRATEFUL TO MARYKNOLL for my nine years of seminary training and six years as a priest in Guatemala.

A few months ago, I received a letter from Guatemala inviting me to the inauguration of a school named in my honor. After leaving San Antonia Huist 44 years ago, I returned this past February. Marsha (my wife of 33 years) and I went for an amazing celebration. Local people videoed much of the occasion and edited it on-line in a 25-minute format, available at VIMEO.com/2133 2796.

The whole process started me thinking of those long-ago years and the years since.

In the seminary, I kept the rule and was religiously devoted but I was not a student. I slept a great deal in class, which makes me wonder why they ever kept me. I was not interested in philosophy or theology. I did enjoy the novitiate year, was attentive to the training, and only wish I had been capable of taking it more deeply.

For the summer vacation after second theology, I asked permission of our wonderful rector, Fr. Tom Malone, to attend a class in "cooperativism" at St. Francis Xavier University in Nova Scotia, Canada, where I finally found a subject that interested me. For the first time, I realized there was a political, social, and economic system other than capitalism. My eyes were opened. I had inadvertently found a practical spiritual life that I could base my priesthood and mission life on.

The second subject that gained my attention was in fourth year dogma, when our teacher (I don't recall his name), introduced us to

Fr. Pierre Teilhard de Chardin. It touched my mind and my soul. I am grateful for these wonderful gifts.

After a total of six years in Guatemala, the last three in San Antonia Huista with two very dedicated Maryknoll nuns, I joined in support of the revolutionary movement, Las Fuerzas Armadas Rebeldes (FAR). After a betrayal by a priest in the movement, I was told to leave Guatemala. I went to Mexico, where after four months I was arrested and sent back to the United States. I then began a two-year lecturing tour around the country, basically comparing the war against Vietnam to the war against Guatemala.

In October of 1968, Catherine (formerly a Sister in San Antonia Huista, Sister Leonor) returned to the United States and joined the travel and lecture tour. We married that year and remained married for seven years. After divorcing, we both went back to school. Before that, we participated in an antiwar action against the madness of napalm and its manufacturer, Dow Chemical Co.

For the last 35 years, I have been in Long Beach, Calif., happily working as a psychotherapist, learning ever more about myself, life, and spirituality. I could have done none of this without the foundation Maryknoll gave me.

Special thanks to Fr. Al Fedders, Fr. Joe Grassi, Fr. Bill O'Leary, Fr. Mike Thompson, Ed Stroud, Joe Dooley, Fr. Dan McLaughlin, Fr. Bob Crawford, Fr. Ed Davis, Joe Davis, Fr. Bill Woods, Fr. Jerry Hammond, and so many others who have had such a powerful influence on my life.

Thank you, Maryknoll!!

❑

In both his marriages to wonderful women, they and Art were not inspired to have children. However they feel they have many kids, here and in Guatemala. In 1992 Art published the book *With Eyes to See: A Journey from Religion to Spirituality* (Stillpoint, 1992).

The Continuity of Life:
A Little Patch of Green

Bill Mersch ('71)

INITIALLY I WAS NOT GOING TO SUBMIT AN ARTICLE for this project, but after reading a recent article in the *Boston Globe* by James Carroll, I thought I would share a few thoughts. Carroll was a Paulist priest for a number of years, but then left to pursue writing and teaching. In the article he writes about how the change from analog to digital time keeping is really a reflection of how our society operates today. One of his most salient points is an example of how society, which used to look at life as "a continuity," an ongoing process, now views life as "episodic," in bits and bytes. We have come to chop everything up into small pieces, whether it is the daily news or our twitter relationships. As Carroll says, we have moved from the analog clock that has a face and a history to a faceless timepiece.

As I reflected on the Carroll article, it dawned on me that I had in one sense thought of my three years with Maryknoll as an experience I had over 40 years ago with little or no impact on my life today. It was a "bit" experience I had at one point in my life but not an integral part of my personal continuity, my history. But then I realized the hand of time may sweep along into the future, but the present and future are not real without the past. In that light, Maryknoll profoundly impacted who, what, and where I am today. I realized that, in addition to Maryknoll's influence on my family and work, I came to understand how the three short years of experience at Maryknoll helped to lay the foundation for my ongoing intellectual and spiritual development, the belief system I have today.

A recent article by Nicholas Nash, professor of divinity at Cambridge University, called "Teaching or Commanding," presents a view that Vatican II helped us to recognize "that all Christians are called to a lifelong learning in the Spirit." Maryknoll helped me to question many things and in fact taught me that, in the end, my conscience must be the guide for how to live my life. Too often the Church has been viewed as a commander rather than a teacher. The Maryknoll environment was definitely a teaching environment. It taught me that "doubt" is acceptable and necessary, because without doubt you cannot have faith. The realm that goes beyond empirical facts cannot be blindly accepted simply based on someone else's thinking and analysis. Everyone must develop his or her own faith and beliefs. If there are 6.5 billion people on this planet, there are 6.5 billion belief systems. We all must find our own way, which means developing an individual relationship with God.

Over the 40-plus years since I left Maryknoll, I have had many hours to think about life. I have formulated what for me are beliefs that I can live with and guide my actions. Without Maryknoll I know my thinking would have taken a different direction, but it did not, and I am thankful. Being somewhat of a loner while in Maryknoll, I allowed myself to do a fair amount of reading and thinking, which has carried over until today. I guess this is the result of training in philosophy and a lot of quite time at the novitiate.

Where has it led me? As the Existentialists say, what gives meaning to life is death. I also believe that what gives meaning to living is the fact that we are fallible. Everything we do is an effort to overcome our limitations and reach for something more, a higher goal, and a betterment of who we are. We are never satisfied with the status quo. There is always the past record to beat or another barrier to overcome—all part of the evolutionary process. I also believe this is one of the foundations of Christianity and Maryknoll. We would not need either if everything was perfect. Everything would be realized. In fact, I can only believe in Christianity when I look at it through the lens of evolution. When I entered Maryknoll, I did not think it was going to lead me on an intellectual journey, but it has, and for this I am grateful. Maryknoll has taught me that it is not only good to question everything, but it is necessary, as we continue the evolutionary process.

In addition to developing my philosophy of life, Maryknoll

helped me to develop very good friends. To this day my closest friend, a Maryknoll colleague, was the best man at my wedding and a godparent to my son. This same friendship helped me to find a job in business and to stay in close contact with other members of the extended Maryknoll family. Without having entered Maryknoll I would never have moved back to Boston, met my wife of 40 years, gone to graduate school, or raised a family. Although not directly related, I am convinced my Maryknoll experience moved me in the direction of volunteering and helping those in need.

On a final note, over the past year I have had the opportunity of visiting Maryknoll as a part of the Centennial Planning Group. During my visits I have met many active as well as retired priests and Brothers and listened to many stories of their work around the world. It was inspiring to hear stories of dedication and hardship from China, Africa and Latin America. The March/April issue of *Maryknoll* magazine has an article about Father Charlie Cappel, entitled called "A Patch of Green," where he says that his prime mission experience was to leave "a little patch of earth more beautiful than when I came. That's enough for me." From hearing the stories of these dedicated people, I know that Father Cappel is not alone in sowing a "patch of green." I hope that my Maryknoll experience also helped me to leave a little patch of green. To all those who touched my life who are a part of Maryknoll family—they go way beyond those I personally have met and known—I want to thank you.

❑

Bill and his wife, Sandy, live in Groton, Mass. They have a son and two granddaughters. After Maryknoll, Bill obtained an MEd at Northeastern University and an MS from Rivier College. He has worked as a counselor and in human resources for hospitals in the Boston area, as well as at Digital Equipment Corporation, Compaq Computer, and Liberty Mutual Insurance. Additionally, he has volunteered for 15 years with Habitat for Humanity.

Men For Others

Bob McGuire ('71)

THE SOCIETY ALUMNI COORDINATING COMMITTEE requested that Maryknoll alumni submit articles on Maryknoll's influence in their lives and the men responsible for it. In response to that request, this article is submitted. Personally, I never desired to publish anything and never have (except numerous required and mandated official reports) . Upon reflection, I realize that without Maryknoll and the men mentioned in this article, my life would have turned out much differently. Therefore, limited as it may be, this is one man's perspective.

I was fortunate to have two great parents who gave me my "moral compass," and two great brothers who continue to keep me honest. The Holy Family and Presentation Sisters reinforced their training and put it in a faith and spiritual context. The Jesuits trained me to be a critical thinker and to articulate thoughts, concepts, and beliefs. Two of my superior Army officers and close friends taught me the concepts, skills, and reality of command and leadership. Tools I had to use daily in the U.S. Drug Enforcement Agency (DEA). (Note: Whether you are in the military in a war zone or a DEA agent in some U.S city, when you kick in a door, you go to war! There is no difference between the house of a terrorist or a drug dealer, except geographical location. Getting shot, stabbed, or wounded, while attempting an arrest, still means you are just as injured, crippled, or dead! The principles of leadership and command, in fighting the war on terror or the war on drugs, are exactly the same. Command means responsibility and no excuses—just what Maryknoll has always taught!)

Daily, as I shave and am forced to look at my mug in the mirror,

I have no illusions. Abraham Lincoln spoke of our "better angels"; I am fully capable of being a "lesser angel"! Given the right conditions, there is no atrocity or evil deed beyond my imagination. At these moments, I take the words of Saint Augustine to heart, "If, but for the grace of God, go I." The men of Maryknoll were the instruments of God's grace in my life. In addition to the men mentioned below, my classmates, in particular, made that grace real. All much smarter and more talented than I, they taught me patience and gave me the help, guidance, and friendship without which I would have flunked out in the first semester of my freshman year! Maryknoll is the finest organization I know, or, have ever been a part. It is truly, a selfless organization focused on others.

The following can be viewed as an idealistic, naïve, exuberant, youthful fantasy. Not so! It is written from the perspective of a former Maryknoll priest, Army Airborne (paratrooper) chaplain, and, DEA special agent and Enforcement Group supervisor. Maryknoll is not, and never has been, Camelot, Shangri La, or Paradise. It is a society of finite men, with human frailties and weaknesses, living committed lives dedicated to others. They are tough men, with big hearts, gentle souls, sharp minds, and a laser-like focus on the needs and welfare of others. The men of Maryknoll live and work in the real world (mostly, the poorest, most under developed areas), where the timid would never go. They believe, to the very core of their being, in God's love, mercy, and redemption. They witness to it through lives of sacrifice and in service to others. One other thing: every Maryknoller I know, has a sense of purpose, a desire for excitement and adventure, and wants a challenge bigger than himself. In a phrase, Maryknollers are purposeful, committed, "adrenaline junkies," living lives of faith and commitment! Maryknollers contemplate a lot, but contemplatives they were and are not!

Men for others, the essence of Maryknoll. From Day One of a Maryknoller's training, he is told that he is being groomed to serve others—not himself. His life is to be a servant to the poorest of the poor, the voiceless, and the powerless. A man of Maryknoll has no illusions. His comfort, convenience, and self-actualization are not the focus of his training. Candidates do not join Maryknoll to work out their psychological, emotional, and intellectual needs, or, resolve a conflicted personality. They come to serve, give of themselves fully and totally for others, and go to parts of the world most never think of, except during times of tsunamis, earthquakes, hurricanes, wars, and other disasters. Though motivated by faith and spirituality, they are hard men voluntarily going to some of the worst regions of the world. Living lives committed to others.

The "other guy" comes first; you last. A Maryknoller is taught that salvation of his immortal soul rests in his own hands. His job is to insure others can live in dignity, so they can accomplish the salvation of their souls. More than anything, a Maryknoller is trained not to throw roadblocks in the path of those he serves. He is to walk shoulder to shoulder with his fellow man, not in a position of superiority. Maryknollers learn to take complete responsibility for their actions and to freely give power away. Empower others, hold yourself to the highest standards, and, live (not just preach) what you believe. A tall order, but marching orders all Maryknollers freely embrace. Maryknoll's training objectives: get a young man's mind right and focused and his priorities in order. Narcissistic, self-centered, selfish individuals need not apply.

"Gentlemen, work yourselves out of a job. Do not build personal kingdoms and empires. Empower others. Teach by the way you live your life and learn from those to whom you are sent." What a novel concept. Maryknollers learn this from the start and live by it to the end of their lives. A man of Maryknoll learns that God created the world; His Son redeemed it; and His Spirit inspires it. A Maryknoller is but God's instrument, not His surrogate.

In today's world, culture, and society, this is anachronistic. It goes against the grain of the "me" generation: self-interest, self-indulgence, pop psyche (as opposed to good, solid psychological principals and practices), greed, power, status, luxury, etc. A higher good, something bigger than yourself; a mission of sacrifice for others less fortunate—are you crazy! Yep, that's Maryknoll. If you survived Maryknoll's training, you know a few things: you were part of a team, privileged to be standing on the shoulders and sacrifices of better men who went before you, and you were expected to carry on in that same outstanding tradition and spirit of service, sacrifice and dedication to "God's people."

There were no small jobs. Most times, you were never given choices. All jobs were important (even if you did not see it that way), predicated on the greater good and needs of God's Kingdom,

Church, and the Society. Your personal feelings were not important.

You volunteered and always knew you were a man for others, not yourself. In a similar vein, it was drummed into every Maryknoller the standards to which you were held. You represented the Church and the Society. Do not cause scandal and embarrassment to the Society, Church, your family, or yourself—in that order.

God does work in strange ways. All Maryknoll seminarians fully intended to persevere to ordination. All ordained intended to be a "priest for life." Not always the case. Leave it to God to let you know your will may not be His. All of us who were or are Maryknollers know this. But the proof of God working in the world through Maryknoll is found in the lives of all who claim to have ever been a part of it: seminarians, priests, Brothers, or Associates.

Service is the common thread running through all Maryknoller's lives. Aside from those of priests and Brothers, careers in medicine and its related fields, social work, education, coaching, law, the helping professions, government, service-oriented businesses, agriculture, community development, and the like are all populated and influenced by former Maryknollers. The ideals of empowering others, leading by example, working side-by-side with all (not only in positions of power, authority, and privilege), and giving others the credit—not seeking self-adulation, fame, and glory for yourself. This sums up Maryknoll's approach to life and mission and its method of operation. Men for others.

After leaving Maryknoll, I joined the DEA. Several former Maryknoll classmates and alumni had also become DEA special agents, investigators, or intelligence analysts. Without exception, we all knew we were servants of the American people. Our job: give America's children the opportunity to grow up free from drug addiction and its associated dehumanization and violence (give our country's future generation the chance to grow up with a clear head; in a safe environment, free from the drug culture's violence; and, free from the insecurity of living in predatory, drug-infested urban jungles!). Idealistic, yes, but, you have to try! We had left Maryknoll, but Maryknoll had never left us.

I commanded the first DEA Mobile Enforcement Team (MET) (a drug-gang suppression enforcement group and SWAT team), in Los Angeles. Its mission: target and attack the most violent drug organizations in a specific area/community. The Los Angeles MET was different and unique from any other in DEA: it was an agent-driven program. The field agent designed, collaborated with local counterparts, and executed the program. The "street agent" was empowered to make the program work. DEA headquarters (Washington, D.C.) control and interference was kept to an absolute minimum; while the street agent's and local jurisdiction's control, influence, and ideas were maximized. The local jurisdiction's police department identified their major drug problems and the strategies for "cleaning them up." The DEA/ MET came in as a partner, working side-by-side with them; it did not seek credit, but served in any capacity needed to accomplish the overall mission. It was the most successful MET operation in the DEA, thanks to being run by the principles ingrained in all Maryknollers: service, teamwork, empowering others, and not seeking personal credit.

Talk about job satisfaction; nothing can surpass the experience of what little, old, illegal alien grandmothers did in Los Angeles in 1996. They came out of a ghetto apartment building, which MET agents had just raided and arrested over ten violent drug traffickers. They approached the agents. Now these agents were in full raid gear; wearing bullet-proof vests, ballistic helmets with face shields. (They looked more like Star Wars troopers than humans!) With weapons seemingly coming out of every orifice of their bodies, they were most often big, tough men (and, one female special agent)—individuals not to be trifled with! These grandmothers came up, with tears in their eyes, and kissed the agents' hands, saying how grateful they were. For the first time in many years they could now live in peace, knowing that the drug thugs could no longer harm them or their grandchildren. Not one agent had a dry eye; they could only awkwardly (because of all of the equipment they were wearing) return the grandmothers' spontaneous hugs. On this particular day, DEA/MET agents experienced what Maryknoll missioners experience in the far-off mission fields of the world. God graced them (and me) with a blessing from some of His most humble, downtrodden, and persecuted (by drug traffickers). Being men and women for others (even if you carry a badge and gun, rather than a crucifix) has its rewards!

As far as working yourself out of a job: the Los Angeles MET team went through a total of four commanders, yet remained the most successful MET program in DEA for ten years, until the MET program was discontinued in 2006. At the time of its deactivation, it was a better, more productive, effective, and highly trained unit than at any time in its history. It had deployed to over forty drug-infested cities, neighborhoods and jurisdictions, and assisted in "taking back the streets" for the good people living there. The reason: it remained focused on empowering others (both the "street" agents and the communities to whom they were sent); teamwork (walking side-by-side with local counterparts, not just "calling the shots"), and never seeking personal credit (be generous in recognizing the accomplishments of others).

Maryknollers know God has a sense of humor. Who would have thought Maryknoll's training, concepts, and ideas would be responsible for the success of one of DEA's most innovative antidrug, law enforcement programs. The things you learn, sitting in theology class, trying to stay awake, contemplating, "being qua being" and "the uncaused cause"!

Maryknoll's secret weapon is the outstanding individuals chosen to teach and form its candidates. Three men, Fathers Thomas Wilcox, M.M., Richard H. "Bull" Allen, M.M., and John E. Bergwall, M.M., epitomized Maryknoll's formation program. All preached little, prayed much in private (on their knees, in the darkest shadows and corners of the chapel), and lived consistent, congruent lives of discipline, spirituality, and faith. They never demanded more from others, than they did of themselves. In formation you always knew they were the adult. Once ordained, they welcomed you as an equal and full member of the Society they absolutely loved. By observing these men you learned how to lead, serve, and take responsibility for your own actions and decisions. They were quick to forgive, slow to anger, and always demanded unwavering fidelity to duty, the Church, Society, and vows. They led from the front, by the lives they lived.

Tom Wilcox: priest, scholar, athlete, troubleshooter. Tom wanted to go to the missions, but was assigned instead to study and then teach Latin in Maryknoll's seminary system. Personally disappointed, he did his duty. He was a kind and generous teacher (who would pass you, if you worked hard, did your homework, and, got "close" to the correct translation!) and was an outstanding athlete who could have played professional soccer. Instead he was

Father Bernard Meyer, M.M., and Bishop James E. Walsh, M.M.

a magnificent coach for many of us. Your very best was always demanded, but mistakes, human frailty and failings were quickly acknowledged and forgiven. From the outset, when playing on one of "Father Tom's" teams you quickly learned that playing on a Maryknoll team was not a right but a privilege, and responsibility had to be be earned. The athletic field was merely an extension of the classroom. You either performed in class or you did not play. You were always representing Maryknoll and the team. You were expected to be disciplined always, to give your maximum effort and ability, and never embarrass Maryknoll or the team. (On a personal note: When I was going through the Army's Jump School [paratrooper] training and the DEA Academy [even though I was no longer a Maryknoll priest], I knew I was representing Maryknoll, my classmates, and the priesthood. Failure was not an option! My failure would make them and the Church look bad. An unrealistic perspective, maybe, but it sure motivated me not to quit! The lessons taught and modeled by Tom Wilcox are not soon forgotten!) Tom was often, quietly, called upon by the Society to solve sensitive problems. He never spoke of these assignments; he just unobtrusively did his duty and assisted fellow Maryknollers in need or trouble. Late in his career, he was sent to China, following in the footsteps of Maryknoll's first China missioner, Bishop James Edward Walsh, M.M.

Disciplined, deeply spiritual, private, and inwardly reflective describe Tom Wilcox. Always there to help, never asking for anything except one's very best, and completely understanding of the human condition. These qualities made him an outstanding priest, mentor, role model, and cherished friend. By the way, he would be embarrassed to have these accolades made public. Humility was Tom Wilcox' stock and trade! But his contributions to Maryknoll are immeasurable and should be recognized. He has always been a man for others, working in the shadows, never asking anything for himself.

Dick Allen spent his entire life in formation, and administration and as a confidant to many in the society. His gifts of wisdom, insight, bluntness, and total dedication to the Society were without question. He had a master's degree in biology and was assigned to teach in the seminary system (he would have much preferred a mission assignment!). A deep thinker, a serious and practical theologian, the Bull always put things in perspective. No pie-in-the-sky solutions for Dick Allen: face facts and reality, admit mistakes, and move on and solve the problem. He once told me, "Having the sweet love of Jesus in your heart and on your lips is fine. Just make sure, a man also has food in his belly." Always practical, who could argue with that?! For the Bull, theory was fine for the classroom, but life required real solutions. One did not pontificate endlessly in the Bull's presence! The Bull and Maryknoll make faith and spirituality practical! The Bull was always there for those of us who were less than stellar students, scholars, and intellects. Strong backs and weak minds were OK with the Bull as long as you were giving it your all—he had no time for slackers, phonies, or prima donnas! He could always put things in perspective and give you confidence and encouragement, even when things seemed their bleakest. A big, gruff, tough man in appearance, in reality he was a gentle, sensitive bear. He could read men like a book and he had no use for pretenders. He always looked out for the little guy, the individual who had problems fitting in, and the good-hearted soul who was often misunderstood.

Many superiors and others sought Father Allen's advice, counsel, and insights before making decisions. You never learned this from Dick, only after the fact from those who had sought it. Every organization needs someone who quietly works behind the scenes to help it accomplish its mission—a "fixer." For many years, the Bull was that man. When the Society had a problem, the Bull was thrown into the breach, got the problem solved, and was then sent on to fix some other problem/issue. He died too young, at a time when the Society was going through many changes. His death left a vacuum in the Society. To those of us he helped and mentored, he was a giant of a man and priest to be emulated! An example of Dick Allen's depth was you would find him, at odd hours, sitting in the very back, darkest corner of the chapel, reading his breviary, praying, and quietly reflecting. You would never find him in the first pew, under a light, or being in any way conspicuous. His sermons were short, his faith deep, and his love of the Church and Maryknoll unquestioned. He always served, never complained, and taught many of us the reality of being a strong, competent, compassionate priest. He always subjugated his own will for that of God and Maryknoll.

John Bergwall was a World War II Navy veteran, medical doctor, Maryknoll missioner, friend, mentor, and role model. Born in Hartland, Wisc., the son of a medical doctor, he was called right out of high school to serve his country as a sailor during World War II. He came home from war, went to Marquette University, became a medical doctor, and then responded to a vocation to become a Maryknoll missioner. He went through seminary formation and training, got ordained, and was assigned to Tanzania (East Africa), where he came down with multiple sclerosis! After three years in the missions his disease made him unable to continue as a missionary and he was reassigned to formation at Maryknoll College, Glen Ellyn, Ill. The mission's loss, the seminary's gain. When "Bergie" came into our lives, he brought a wicked sense of humor, a courage one often reads about but seldom sees, and an unshakable faith. His counsel was always on point, his optimism contagious, and his dedication to Maryknoll limitless. Though confined to a wheelchair for many, many years, Bergie was a magnet for others. No one ever went to see Bergie for "counseling," only to "visit" him. Right! His "visitors" outnumbered most psychiatrist's practices! His ability to put things into perspective was unique and his quiet faith, awe inspiring. He never criticized, but his "observations" were always dead-on accurate. With a brilliant mind, trapped within a deteriorating body, one could ask, "How could this be?!"

Bergie answered that question by the way he lived his life in faith and resignation to God's will. He always focused on others, never dwelled on his own problems/situation, and always lived a life of joyful faith. I have been fortunate to know many tough, hard, good men in my life, but I have never known one tougher, more committed to their God and Society, or a better friend than Father John E. Bergwall. Though he battled a crippling infirmity for most of his adult life, he daily offered up his sufferings for the success of the Society, the missions, and his many "visitors" with issues and needs. Truly, a man for others!

In conclusion, "Men for Others" summarizes Maryknoll's mission statement. A Society of men, founded by men, doing God's work in some of the most forsaken regions of the world. Its imperfect members are what make it remarkable. Maryknoll is both a concept and reality. It affects all who are, or, have ever been a part of it, with a unique spirit. Service to others, ask not the cost to self, and share God's love to all by the way you conduct your life. Ideals and concepts often preached. Maryknoll, as a Society, actually does it. The priests mentioned above are examples of such men. The rest of us can only be thankful for having had the opportunity to know and be influenced by them.

Today, many are called heroes (not always deservingly so!). For one hundred years, the men of Maryknoll, both individually and as a Society, have lived quiet, heroic lives of self-discipline, sacrifice, and service to others; witnessing to God's love for the world and mankind. Men for Others! I am eternally most grateful that Maryknoll permitted me to be a small part of it for a significant portion of my life.

❑

Ordained in 1971, assigned to Promotion for three years, then went into the Army, as an Airborne (paratrooper) chaplain, serving with the 82nd Airborne, Special Forces, and INSCOM. Resigned from Maryknoll in 1977 and joined the U.S. Department of Justice, Drug Enforcement Administration in 1978, serving as a compliance investigator, special agent, and enforcement group supervisor. Retired from DEA in 1998, was hired by the Southern California Drug Task Force, where I instructed in firearms, tactics, and other related subjects until 2005. In 2005 moved to Idaho, where I volunteer with the U.S. Forest Service and am involved in other community activities.

Entrance into a New World

by Vic Hummert ('67)

Excerpts from Dear Thomas: A Memoir for Thomas Berry,
by Vic Hummert (Amazon/CreateSpace, 2010).

MARYKNOLL SEMINARY was located in Glen Ellyn, Illinois, an affluent suburban town roughly twenty-five miles west of Chicago. The seminary was located on what was formerly a country club and golf course where the infamous Al Capone and other Chicago gangland characters relaxed.

There were nearly 400 students in the seminary at that peak time in the Maryknoll Society's history. Four of us were crowded into one small room with bunk beds.

* * *

In the early 1960s Maryknoll enlarged the accommodations in Glen Ellyn to house the growing numbers who were entering the college seminary. This was before the Second Vatican Council had its revolutionary impact upon the church and interest in clerical religious life began to wane. Today, not one Maryknoll Seminary is functioning as a training center for priests or Brothers. The Maryknoll headquarters and former major seminary in Ossining, N.Y., has been converted into administrative offices and a retirement home for aging priests and Brothers. The Maryknoll Society was once a conduit for large numbers of priests and Brothers to go in service to other nations. Now a different presence is needed, another vehicle of God's goodness to the world. The Maryknoll Lay Missioner program continues to draw numerous applicants, while the clerical doors of Maryknoll seem to be frozen.

Maryknoll is caught in the universal clerical system. Maryknoll cannot disconnect from the church institution that continues to discriminate against women. Dependence upon a celibate, male clerical system is comparable to seeing with one eye, walking on one leg and breathing with only one lung. We can muddle on but with decreased effectiveness in the world.

* * *

I arrived in Glen Ellyn to join students who had already been there for two years. Credits from my two years in Dayton University were recognized and I plunged cold into my third year of college courses. I struggled with a new vocabulary—God became "Yahweh Ebed"—and tried to figure out how to fit in with students who were somewhat clericalized. Third- and fourth-year students wore cassocks and were versed in the Latin language they might have studied for years. I studied Latin in high school, but retained little because the language was of little practical use unless one was studying law or medicine. To overcome this deficit I was thrown in with "Group X," a group older students who had no solid foundation in Latin.

Seminary studies at Glen Ellyn brought me into a meaningful relationship with philosophy. Philosophy was given to me as "the love of wisdom." I felt like a child set free in a candy store. I loved reading the philosophers and wondered if I would have enough time in life to read all of those famous writers. I was determined to sample everybody from Aristotle and Marcus Aurelius down to Schopenhauer (1788–1860), Ludwig Wittgenstein (1889–1951) and the modern philosophers such as Jacques Maritain (1882–1973). I was grateful for the opportunity to devour books in the seminary library. It was in Maryknoll Seminary that I discovered I was an information addict with a deep appreciation for books and magazines.

Glen Ellyn also broadened my view of the world. In March 1961 some of the Boston and New York seminarians of Irish ancestry began discussing among themselves whether St. Patrick's Day would be a holiday. Never having gone much beyond my narrow German Catholic environment, I asked in all innocence, "When is St. Patrick's Day?" Howls of laughter brought home to me that Maryknoll was opening up a new world to me.

* * *

Although I was raised as a Catholic, attended Catholic grammar school and a private Catholic high school, I was not really introduced to the study of sacred scripture until I entered Maryknoll. Our scripture professor, Father John McConnell, gave us small booklets that explained each book of the bible in great detail. While studying Paul's letter to the Corinthians I was stunned to read this passage from First Corinthians: "Do you not know that the temple of God and that the Spirit of God dwells within you?" (I Cor. 3:16) I thought about the passage as I walked over to the window of our seminary room. I glanced out of the window to the east and saw the vast expanse of Chicago. Had I read the passage correctly? I went back to my desk to reread the passage slowly. In September 1960 there were several hundred students in the seminary and 4 million people living in Chicago. Each one of us was a temple of the Spirit. The reading of this profound passage gave me a radically different appreciation of each living being. Scripture began to take root in my heart for the first time.

As a noted scripture scholar Father McConnell was occasionally invited to lecture in other cities. On one such occasion when he had to leave class early to catch a flight he told us to take a piece of paper and draw the ancient temple in Jerusalem, giving all of the different sections—the Wailing Wall, the section reserved for women, and the Holy of Holies. McConnell had taught us that the presence of Jesus in history diminished the importance of the temple but that its importance in biblical history could not be ignored. While we waited for the substitute teacher to arrive, I outlined my recollection of the temple: a few chambers within a larger enclosure.

My esteemed classmate from Boston, Thomas J. Shea, was befuddled by this challenge. Tom placed a large dot on the paper with the heading: View of the Temple from 10,000 Feet. Upon his return, McConnell handed the paper back to his cheeky Bostonian student with a small dot and a large caption overhead: View of a Zero from Fifty Feet.

Another scripture professor, Father William Frazer, taught us not to look upon salvation history in a juridical sense of Jesus paying a price to save the world. Rather he tried to have us accept a "mystical understanding" of a God of Love taking on flesh to teach us as a God who lived among the people and continues to this day since "the reign of God is within you." Father Frazier's approach is embodied in a book written by Francis Xavier Durrwell, a teacher

Living and working in Hong Kong

he studied with in Europe: *The Resurrection: A Biblical Study.*
Durrwell writes about salvation as a mysterious, loving event in
history.

Another professor who had a profound influence on me was Father George Pfister. With a background in physics, Father Pfister was brought back from mission work in Africa to teach in the seminary. He, like many of the missionaries who were brought home to teach, was unhappy about returning to the United States.

Before entering Maryknoll George Pfister was unwittingly a participant in the Manhattan Project, the innocent-sounding yet catastrophic program launched in August 1942 to develop our first atomic bomb. Father Pfister never expressed any pride, however, at being part of such a deadly endeavor.

* * *

On November 21, 1962, my classmates and I were "professed" as clerical members of Maryknoll and were given black cassocks and a cincture to wear around our waist. That Investiture Day was my formal introduction into the Maryknoll family.

In 2009 I still maintain contact with several friends who are still in the Maryknoll Society, and with a larger number who have moved on to different callings in the world. The Catholic church is my spiritual mother and Maryknoll is still my extended family. I am eternally grateful to all who have been so supportive to me since 1960. I do not think I will ever "leave" Maryknoll. Roselyn accepts that relationship because Maryknoll associates have appreciated her as my wife since 1998.

The two years in Glen Ellyn went quickly and I found myself with a bachelor's degree in philosophy. When I joined Maryknoll two years earlier I had to reawaken a lounging brain. I had been away from formal education since leaving Dayton University in 1955. I had to "retool" myself after a five-year hiatus. I checked out Mortimer Adler's *How to Read a Book*. One of Adler's conclusions about higher education was, "If at the end of our formal education we do not have the desire to continue reading and studying for the rest of our lives, then our education has been a failure."

After two years of philosophy studies at Glen Ellyn I had already developed a sense of curiosity that continues into my seventh decade of life. I have accumulated more books than I will read for the rest of my days. I am clearly a bookaholic. I never enter a bookstore unless my aim is to pick out one specific volume to peruse.

From Glen Ellyn Maryknoll sent us for a year of spiritual training and introduction to Maryknoll history at a novitiate in Bedford, Massachusetts. We lived that year in a converted dairy barn that was once owned by the Boston diocese. The most memorable moment of 1962 was the Cuban missile crisis, but our strict novice master would not allow us to have radios or access to a television; nor was there a newspaper to read. Entombed in this irrelevant monastic setting, we learned via that telephone that worried Catholics were then lining up for confession outside of churches in New York City, fearing a nuclear exchange between the Soviet Union and the USA. We had no idea whatsoever that the second nuclear catastrophe in history was on the horizon. A narrow spirituality honed us into believing nuclear warfare was beyond our control.

After a year I was pleased to move on from Bedford. The next phase of our training was a four-year program of theological studies at Maryknoll's major seminary in Ossining, N.Y.

❑

Vic and Roselyn Hummert, 122 Rosedale Dr., Lafayette, LA 70508. Email: vic@vichummert.org.

A Continuing Quest

Ron DuBois ('63)

TWO COURSES AT MARYKNOLL SEMINARY planted seeds in me for a continuing quest for understanding. Joe Grassi's New Testament class challenged us to take responsibility for our own learning. Joe didn't lecture. Instead, he assigned several articles for reading for each class. Then during class he facilitated a discussion based on those readings. Of course, Joe participated in the discussion but the burden was on us to share what we had learned.

Colleagues may be surprised at the second class that influenced me greatly. It was Larry Vaughan's ecclesiology class. Larry was not a great theologian nor a great lecturer. But what he did was to reject the scholastic Latin text approved for the course and substitute Yves Congar's *Lay People in the Church* as the required text. There we were in 1962, while the first session of the Second Vatican Council was going on, learning from the theologian who most significantly influenced the *Dogmatic Constitution on the Church* (Lumen Gentium). Those two classes have led to my continuing quest to understand Scripture and the reality of the Church. And they have helped lead to my involvement in Voice of the Faithful and in efforts to reform the Church in light of Vatican II.

❏

Ron and his wife, Kay Doherty, live in Braintree, Mass. A retired management consultant, Ron continues his service by managing the Chi Rho Fund. He is also a member of the board of Voice of the Faithful. Kay has three daughters and she and Ron delight in sharing in the grandparenting of twins Rosalie and Jenson.

My Life and the Influence
of Maryknoll Training on It

Bob O'Neil ('68)

I HAVE BEEN A CLINICAL SOCIAL WORKER for the past 43 years. I have been specializing in the treatment of adolescents and adults with poor impulse control. I have no plans to retire as I enjoy my work and I never put much value in personal financial security. So I am not in a position to retire.

In the past 50 years, it's just that I have not been religious since I left Maryknoll Seminary. I don't want to offend anyone who has spent their life relying on God for their sustenance and well-being. I believe I have been spiritual and my spirituality has grown stronger in recent years. My definition of spirituality is humility combined with the courage and freedom to follow your gut feelings. This is the state of mind I am in when I feel most spiritual and closest to God.

My relationship with God has gone through a metamorphosis. While I was in the seminary, my image of God was that he was harsh and relentless in his demands of me. And if I failed him, I would be punished for all eternity. As a result, I was always feeling guilty no matter how hard I tried to be good. Also, I believed I needed to rely on God to help me through difficult times in my life. As a result, I blamed God when things did not work out for me. These attitudes defined my relationship with God until age 29. I woke up one day and decided my relationship with God is not working for me. I gave up on God. And I decided that I would begin to rely on myself to make decisions. And I would take responsibility for my actions. And I would take the blame for my actions. This allowed me to become honest with myself and to learn from my mistakes. As time went on, I felt more competent and my self-esteem improved.

When I was 42 years old, I became involved in a situation where my relationship with God was challenged. I was asked to define my relationship with God on a human level. My response was that I was afraid of him. I was then asked to make a list of the qualities of this God who so intimidated me. Again I was to use human qualities to describe this God. When I did this, I could easily visualize why God would appear so terrifying to me. It was an image of a very harsh God. Then I was asked to create a God utilizing the type of human qualities that I could live with. Well, I did this. And when I went to sleep that night, I awoke about 4 A.M. to the most blissful experience of feeling connected to God. This encounter stayed with me until 12 noon. And this state of mind, this feeling of being connected to God has been available to me for the rest of my life. It is available to me on recall whenever I take the time to contemplate God. I don't always have the time available that I would like. And while this is happening, I am filled with a sense of inner peace. Until now, I have never spoken of this experience to anyone. Because, quite frankly, I don't understand why this happens nor do I understand what is happening to me when this takes place.

I didn't leave Maryknoll Seminary in the best emotional state of mind. For this I offer no apology, nor shame. If I were to take the time to explain myself, I believe my life would be a story of inspiration. I would have no problem doing this except for the fact it would be inappropriate in this context to do so. Since I left the seminary, I became enmeshed in Freudian, or more commonly entitled, psychodynamic psychological theory. My professor in graduate school was Sophia Freud throughout my training. She is Sigmund Freud's granddaughter. And the rest of my professors were psychoanalysts from the Boston Psychoanalytic Institute. I went to Simmons College, School of Social Work. At the time we shared the same professors as the Harvard Medical Interns who were in training to be psychiatrists. One of the professors was Dr. Senrad, who was legendary in his lifetime. Interestingly, he grew up on a farm in Kansas.

It's been over fifty years since I left Maryknoll Seminary. And I have come to believe our Ego Ideal is formed by age six. So I

Maryknoll High School (The Venard)
Clarks Summit, Pennsylvania

brought to Maryknoll Seminary at age 13 an already formed personality as I believe all our classmates did. How much influence Maryknoll has had on my development is something I have contemplated long and hard over the past few months since the topic was first raised. The answer I have arrived at is simply, I don't know. But I will tell you this: I felt loved the whole time I lived at Maryknoll. The priests that taught us, my classmates, and the whole atmosphere was permeated with love, goodness, and sensitivity. I feel I entered the seminary as a bull in a china shop and the priests and fellow students guided me along in a manner that I could not have possibly handled in any other atmosphere. To me, the "Maryknoll Spirit" did exist and had a positive effect on all of us. I was good in sports activities. This sustained my self-esteem as I grew slowly to develop better manners. I certainly must have been irritating to many due to my lack of socialization skills during the early years in the seminary. But everyone was so patient and kind to me. All I remember was this kindness.

In the fall of 2008, I decided I would take it upon myself to organize a 50-year high school class reunion of 1959. From the class yearbook I had the names of classmates and knew where they had been raised. While it was easy to contact several of my classmates who remained close to where they had lived when they were in the seminary, there didn't appear to be much enthusiasm to get together. Also, the majority could not be located. And as luck would have it, the Centennial with all the contacts suddenly popped up two years later. Even though 50 years have gone by, I can clearly visualize how all of you looked at age 19 or 20. I saved all the class pictures during the Venard years and freshman year at Glen Ellyn. And I plan to bring them with me to the Welcome Home Event in September. My years at Maryknoll Seminary were meaningful in a most positive manner. There are many classmates with whom I have meaningful memories.

My life certainly has been a journey. I have accomplished the goals I set for myself—goals I had hoped to accomplish with my life. Even though it has been over 50 years since we parted, it seems to me that it is like yesterday when I last saw all of you. I am looking forward to meeting everyone and hearing how everyone else's life has turned out. I would like to thank all of you who have taken the time to organize this celebration in September.

❏

Bob O'Neil lives in Rhode Island. He can be reached via email at poe1raven @aol.com.

Three Ideas:
A Tongue-in-Cheek Recollection

Thomas M. Whaling ('61)

MY **RELIGIOUS JOURNEY** started early in life. My father, who was a graduate of the San Francisco Minor Seminary (St. Joseph's) and of the Major Seminary (St. Patrick's), often brought to my attention the many associates he had who were priests and bishops, who often visited our house. My mother simultaneously took me to daily Mass from the third grade through the eighth grade at a Dominican Parish (St. Dominic's) in Eagle Rock, which is in the corner of northeastern Los Angeles. She constantly told me about certain saints who had a vocation and, if they had not accepted "The Gift," they would have been doomed to the eternal fire. I've often wondered whose theology supported this admonition.

At Confirmation at St. Dominic's, one of the adults had given me a book entitled *Men of Maryknoll*. Later that same year, a tall, black-haired, Maryknoll priest, named Father Kelleher, preached at St. Dominic's. I was hooked (maybe hoodwinked, since I hadn't a clue about the sacrifices of a vocational life). Resultantly, the Dominicans lost out to Maryknoll because the tall, dark, and handsome priest told a much more inspirational story—not the hellfire and brimstone scenario often preached by the Order of Preachers.

I was taken by my father to Maryknoll Mountain View (Los Altos) in September 1947. The seminary buildings, now used as a retirement facility for Maryknoll priests and Brothers, look exactly the same today as they did when I entered in my freshman high school year. Often when I drive the 280 Freeway in the Silicon Valley, I look up and see the Chinese bell tower. It is always a welcome sight. However, the big difference today is that there are expensive houses and an attractive county park occupying the bucolic landscape of cows and oak trees dotting the rolling hills that we seminarians traversed each day in the late 1940s.

I spent two years there until I realized what God allowed me to "lust after." Frankly, because my parents were not prone to discuss the sexual appetites and because the young guys at the seminary (who loved to discuss the subject) weren't a cornucopia of valid information, I did not have a clear picture of what was transforming my being. The only information I remember on this topic was Father Manning telling us at the Santa Clara railroad station, when we were leaving in the summer of 1949, that we would be the object of girls' desires because we were "forbidden fruit." I have from time to time pondered on that limited sexual discussion and wondered what is fantasy and what is reality. For most of my life, I haven't made the intellectual connection.

* * *

Seminary life was spiritually inspirational. It was a time of many World War II veterans in the seminary. I do believe I might have stayed in the seminary and tried to become a priest, if I had fully understood what was going on inside me. But alas, I found a different life. I had seven children, was divorced, fell away from the church, and went on a religious odyssey that caused me to temporarily become a Pentecostal, Hedonist, then a fundamentalist. I finally found my way back to the Catholic Church and I now subscribe to the *NCR* mentality, greatly influenced by women and men who no longer see the church as an institutional service organization. These are men and women who were greatly influenced by Vatican II and the work of Dorothy Day and the Latin American Liberation theologians.

* * *

My most profound Maryknoll–life connection in this latter time was meeting Father Roy Bourgeois, M.M., in El Salvador in 2010 and discussing his theological view on women's ordination and the adventures in Fort Benning, Ga. On that trip, while experiencing the shame of the oppression of the poor by some of the Catholic clergy and the class-conscious upper society in El Salvador, I saw how our U.S foreign policy benefited transnational corporations. I also had an earlier Maryknoll experience when I listened to Blase Bonpane, whom I had invited to talk at my "NOW" Democratic Club in Orange, Calif., in 1970. He has been even more inspirational, while hearing his voice on radio station KPFK. Two Maryknoll priests, whom I have an acquaintance with from seminary days, who have continued with Maryknoll, are Fathers Wayman Deasy and Michael Callanan from the Bay Area in California. They both labored in Africa. Currently, they are on an e-mail list that sparks my former Maryknoll seminarians from the West Coast. The writings cover the entire spectrum of Catholicism.

While in El Salvador in March 2010, I had a very impactive experience relating to the martyrdom of the two Maryknoll nuns. I will quote from my 2010 newsletter:

"The most moving experience of my journey was to visit and pray at the grave sites of the two Maryknoll and one Ursuline nuns who were murdered; and then later to sing at the Maryknoll Memorial Chapel in Santiago Nonualco, the location where they, along with Jean Donovan, were murdered.

I still hear the beautiful voice of one of our leaders, Mary Anne Perrone, as she led us in Bob Dufford's 'Be Not Afraid.' The words of the song call out for written transcription as the St. Louis University Jesuit's harmony comes naturally to us Catholics."

Be Not Afraid

You shall cross the barren desert,
   But you shall not die of thirst.
You shall wander far in safety
   Though you do not know the way.
You shall speak your words in foreign lands
   And all will understand.
You will see the face of God and live.
   Refrain
   Be not afraid. I go before you always,
   Come follow me, and I will give you rest.
         If you pass through raging waters in the sea
         You shall not drown.

If you walk amid the burning flames
   You shall not be harmed.
If you stand before the pow'r of hell
   And death is at your side,
Know that I am with you through it all.
   Refrain
Blessed are the poor,
   For the Kingdom shall be theirs,
Blest are you that weep and mourn
   For one day you shall laugh.
And if wicked tongues insult and hate you
   All because of me,
Blessed, blessed are you!"
   Refrain

This hymn was the closing action of our group's last re-flection. It still resonates in my mind. I was privileged to stay another day and that ended in a night at a restaurant, El Rincon de Chile, where service, food, and song were an out-standing adventure.

Some scenes and events that stand out were: the priest in the Chalatenango Cathedral rectory (where the nuns lived before they were murdered), who said 'Romero was con-fused.' (I was led to believe his statement was a euphemistic spin on the Church's antagonism toward Liberation Theology and real justice for the poor)."

Maryknoll has had a substantial influence on my life, and I thank the Lord for that gift. I am still proud to be associated with Maryknoll.

❏

A cradle Catholic, Thomas was formerly educated at Catholic schools throughout his entire life. However, he did attend various courses at Long Beach State (master's) and UCLA (law). His bachelor's degree in philosophy is from Santa Clara University and his Juris Doctor is from another Jesuit institution, Loyola University of Los Angeles. A member of the California State Bar since 1965, he is now retired.

Uncle Bill

Christopher Gallant

A FEW YEARS BACK, during a visit to Maryknoll with Bill [Murphy. '71], I remarked, "I think I finally understand you." Recently, Bill asked me to elaborate on what I meant by that. Here is my very abridged story of how I came to finally understand Bill.

Bill, or "Uncle Bill," as I've always called him, is not, in the literal sense, my uncle. As my mother's brother's late wife's sister's second husband, Bill is pretty far down the line on the list of people I'm calling if I ever need a kidney transplant. However, Bill has always been there, as a close family friend, an admired personal mentor, and a trusted and respected confidant; he is every bit my uncle as any blood relative. He's substantially older, so "cousin" doesn't cut it.

Growing up, Bill was something of an enigma to me. Here was a former Catholic priest appreciative of other faiths, open to debating all sides of all arguments on my own faith, always laughing the loudest at the table, and—when I was older—up for sharing a few drinks. I often find myself detailing the intricacies of my school, my work, or my life with Bill. And he does not ask out of politeness, but rather out of genuine curiosity. He is markedly different from the stoic, aloof, and sometimes single-minded priests I interact with at Mass. Surely, I have always thought, Bill is an anomaly in the Catholic Church.

Then, after two decades of believing Bill was the lone riffraff of the Catholic Church, I came to Maryknoll, where Bill introduced me to an entire community, whom he affectionately referred to as the rabble-rousers of the Church. During my short visit, I met a number of Bill's friends and former colleagues, argued about religion, delved deep into the history of Maryknoll, and had some great laughs along the way. Somewhere during that visit, it occurred to me that Bill wasn't an anomaly, but rather the product of a wonderful community of down-to-earth, friendly, intellectually curious, and compassionate people, who seemed to care more for helping others than for preaching; more for helping people search for answers than for providing them; and more about each other than themselves. Finally, I had unlocked the mystery of Bill.

That day I also developed for Bill—which I have never shared with him—a deep respect for making the bold decision to leave such a community, one to whom he had dedicated nearly his entire life. A decision that most certainly did not come lightly but that was surely met with the excitement, passion for life, and desire for exploration that this community so intrinsically embodies.

I applaud Bill and all of you for your dedication to Maryknoll, the church, to the people of the world, and to each other. God bless you.

❑

Christopher Gallant lives in Manhattan with his wife, Laura. He often travels to Massachusetts to visit family and friends in the Boston area, including his Uncle Bill.

Multiple Lenses

Peter Loan ('72)

MARYKNOLL'S BIGGEST IMPACT ON ME, the one that has lasted through so many years, was its gracing me with multiple lenses with which to view the world around me. By "lenses," I mean the way we size up situations or frame issues by drawing on our past experiences, on the patterns we have become used to, and all the biases born of family and cultural influences, of fears and of roads we have selected, neglected, or rejected. The multiplication of lenses began, of course, with breakfast readings at Glen Ellyn. While the value of any particular reading might be debated (George Putnam was certainly happy to share his commentary whenever he proctored breakfast), still the message was clear: how one encountered (or brought, depending on one's theological orientation) Christ among (or to) various cultures depended largely on the cultural lenses through which people viewed reality. Encountering and supporting the People of God varied greatly from Canton to the Beni to Usukuma. Matteo Ricci's position with respect to the Chinese rites issue at the turn of the seventeenth century was a result of his looking deeply through the lens of Chinese culture.

Here are some proverbial lenses that have helped me reflect on the way that my association with Maryknoll has shaped my life.

A single conversation across the table with
/ a wise man is worth a month's study of books.
– Chinese proverb

The presence of so many wise men and women in Maryknoll has been a blessing for me. Remarkably, many of the insights into the dynamics of the early church from Joe Grassi, into human behavior from Gene Kennedy, into how church affairs developed historically and theologically from Bill McCarthy and Bill Frazier, into how to listen critically and ask good questions from Carl Bauer, into practical ways of living one's faith from Tom Cronin— insights that remain with me today.

Wisdom walked the fields, as well. Many Maryknollers became wise through their faithfulness and their attempts both to bring and to find God at the intersection of American and East African culture. I was blessed to have as mentors both Bill Sweeney, who knew the Irish psyche so well, and Art Wille, who knew Julius Nyerere so well! Many others in their goodness, decency, and sacrifices became examples for me of how wisdom comes of perseverance and reflection. Phil Sheerin, Dan Zwack, Ron Hart, Anita McGovern, Mike Kirwen, Caesar Quinn, Dave Stang, Herb Gappa, Dan Ohmann, and many others are included here.

> *If you want happiness for a lifetime, help someone*
> *else.* – Chinese proverb

The biggest change in my understanding of God, developed during the seminary years and buttressed by missioners in the field, was that His relations with His people are not complicated. In my childhood's Irish-Catholic environment in the 1940s and 1950s, the God I knew was a complicated God. He was all powerful, yet I could manipulate Him through my nine First Fridays, or by waiting for the itinerant preachers who would come to our parish with their plenary indulgences, from Rome, for sure, and from heaven, most likely. God made his dos and don'ts known quite clearly. Guilt hovered, because the don'ts were so attractive. But we could wipe the slate clean and start over again just by being sorry in private! That's complicated.

Maryknoll uncomplicated all this for me, not at once, but over time, through story after story from all over the world of parents' dedication and love for their children; through the village people of Tanzania, who never failed to make space at their tables and in their hearts for strangers; and through my predecessors, Maryknoll men and women whose lives were transformed by East African culture, and who lived Tom Cronin's insight that people were more important than principles.

> *Beyond the mountains there are mountains again.*
> – Haitian proverb

Each rugged mountain presents a great challenge. When we reach the top, we rejoice in our success. But during our lives, challenges never end; we stop responding to them only when our time has come, and by then, if all has gone well, we will have passed along to others the courage to continue facing them.

Mount Lolia, in Tanzania's Mara region, was a sacred place for the Luo and a wonderful symbol of the challenges that missioners faced in the wake of Vatican II. When Dan Zwack and Gerry Pavis listened carefully to the Luo people, they were listening to God among the Luo. Their response to the challenges the Luo faced, crafted in careful consultation with the people who faced these challenges as part of the rhythm of their lives, resulted in an adaptation of traditional Catholic practice much as Jesus had adapted Jewish practices to meet the challenges of His times.

Their short-lived efforts to develop Christian communities steeped in Luo culture rather than in Western culture taught me that each challenge, each mountain, is different and may require a different approach; or like Mount Fuji, there may be many good ways to reach the peak.

Many of the mountains I have climbed have been easier because of the courage that Maryknoll colleagues passed on to me.

If a man does away with his traditional way of
living and / throws away his good customs, he
had better first make certain / that he has some-
thing of value to replace them. – Basuto proverb

The hardest part of managing the changes of Vatican II, as welcome as they were, was the discarding of so much of the traditional way of being in the Church. Unlike the assumption underlying the Basuto proverb, the most important changes were not those personal ones (to observe, or not, this custom or that practice) but the systemic ones, relating to vast cultural, economic, technological, and institutional changes. For example, the notion that the missioner brings Christ to those who don't know Him gives way to the notion that the missioner discovers Christ in those to whom she/he is sent.

This new lens, this new way of looking at how God appears in the world has vast implications for how His people behave with one another, how authority is exercised, how truth is assessed and proclaimed. The mission of Maryknoll, that which required missioners to have feet in at least two cultures, helped mediate the impact of these changes. In my observation, the most joyful of Maryknollers overseas were those who entered most deeply into their new culture, now seeing two or more of the many masks of God.

He who fears something gives it power over him.
– Moorish proverb

We can manipulate the past by re-imagining it to fit our convictions and ensure our comfort. But the future is unknown to us and therefore easy to fear. When Maryknoll sent us into other cultures to learn new languages and customs, we had to face our fears. The experience of facing fear reduces its power over us. I believe that Bill Woods knew this well, as did David Stang's sister Dorothy, and many others, including Roy Bourgeois, who stopped fearing the future because the unknown became commonplace and lost its power to frighten.

Every seed knows its time. – Russian proverb

One hundred years is just a clap in a sea of thunderous applause, and Maryknoll, while deserving such applause at 100, surely is not quite the organization that its founders might have imagined. Nor is its clerical future easy to predict in a world where other economies are rising in relation to the United States. Yet Maryknoll arose at just the right time, when the Church in America needed to look outside itself—thinking to win souls for Christ, but in reality transforming itself as it discovered God in all the places it did not expect Him to be hiding. And though a hundred years is a short time, perhaps this seed of transformation has lodged in our genes, those of us who were and are enamored of Maryknoll, and has become part of our DNA, to grow and spread in ways known not to us, but in faithful response to God's plan.

Do not confine your children to your own learning, for they / were born of another time. – Hebrew proverb

I spent the bulk of my formative years in a gritty housing project in Bridgeport, Conn., where life did not seem as precious as it does now when I glance on my grandchildren, Paris, Mason, and Marissa Grace. We were part of the flotsam and jetsam in World War II's wake, an ethnic patchwork of families reunited after the war, keeping our heads down, looking for opportunities, hoping for a better future.

It was a rough environment. I was bullied, and held up at knife point twice before the age of eleven. I bullied others, too. But for competing graces, I might well have enjoyed a career as a small-time hood.

One of these competing graces was the *Maryknoll* magazine. It came to our little apartment on Success Avenue because my mother's cousin, Frederick Donaghy, was a Maryknoll missioner in China. We met occasionally in the graphics section on the magazine's back cover, and while his world seemed strange and dangerous to this young boy, it also seemed better somehow than the world I knew. The magazine offered another lens by which to view the world, a counter to the grim world I took for granted. When we limit our lenses, we flirt with cynicism, that spiritual disease that predicts a glum or unchanging future, stifling surprise and wonder and assuring that whatever happiness we enjoy will not come from within.

Before taking his life, John Wiggins apologized for recruiting me into Maryknoll. He felt responsible for diverting me from a career in journalism. But by then, I had many lenses with which to view the world. I was not flirting with cynicism; every day was filled with wonder, hope, and endless opportunities to learn something new. Great questions presented themselves endlessly to a mind pried open by the great and varied stories told and retold at breakfast tables, in smoke-filled rooms and on dusty trails by Maryknollers in search of God in the people He loves so well. By His grace through Maryknoll, I have come to embrace diversions in the road.

❑

Peter Loan lives with Ceola, his wife of 39 years, in Hyattsville, Md. Since his retirement from the federal government in 2001, he has been writing and providing training broadly in the area of human resource development. Peter and Ceola delight in two children and three grandchildren, who live nearby in the D.C. metropolitan area.

Lessons Learned

Charlotte Cook (Lay Missioner, '92)

TOO OFTEN WE GO TO OUR MISSION assuming we have all the answers and very quickly learn that we do not. Among the gifts I brought back from my ten years in Kenya as a lay missioner are three bits of wisdom I learned from people with whom I worked.

"You can't tell what we are just by looking at us." I was in Rwanda in April 2002, visiting a young woman I had taught a couple of years earlier. On the anniversary of the day the genocide had started eight years earlier we were talking about the tragic event that resulted in the two of us meeting at St. Kizito School in Nairobi. She and her family had eventually found refuge in Nairobi and I was teaching religion in the secondary school supported by the parish where I was assigned. But on this particular spring day after an anniversary Mass I was asking her questions about the days and events following the death of the president in Kigali. At one point she told me she believed that her mother was Tutsi. I laughed and replied that was impossible, "she's so tiny." That's when Maria looked at me very seriously and said, "You can't tell what we are just by looking at us." I should have known better. During the four years I taught at St. Kizito's I had learned to set aside so many of the assumptions I had made about the parties involved in the genocide and the history that led to it. In her gentle, but firm manner, she reminded me that I still had another lesson to learn.

"We fall down and we get up again." My first ministry in Nairobi was working in a community-based, home-care program for people with AIDS. That was in the days before anti-retrovirals

Tanzania, East Africa

were available to the general public in Kenya, especially the poor. A diagnosis of HIV/AIDS was a death sentence. Agnes was the single mother of three young children. Her family lived in their rural home, leaving Agnes to fend for herself. She was a woman of great faith and a lot of spunk. She was a good mother, caring as best she could for her children while she struggled to stay as healthy as possible. Through our program she was able to get some basic medicines and basic food supplies. She gave back to the community by visiting and supporting other women who were also HIV positive. For several months she had remained fairly healthy but then became ill and needed more medical assistance from our nurses. One day during a visit I remarked that I was sorry she was having this setback. She smiled and replied, "We fall down and we get up again." Agnes did fall down and get up again numerous times after that before the illness finally took her life.

"I am grateful for all of the people I have met as a result of James's condition." James was born with cerebral palsy, the result of a prolonged labor and birth. I had been told by Kenyans working with special needs children that over 50 percent of birth defects could be eliminated with improvements in the birth process. James was not so lucky. On the other hand, James was very lucky that he had the mother he had. I met James and his mother, Alice, when he was five years old. Since James could do nothing for himself, Alice did it for him. James could not talk, could not walk, could not hold eating utensils, could not eat with his hands, could not take care of any of his needs. Alice bathed him, clothed him, fed him, carried him, changed and cleaned him. One of the things James could do was smile and he did that often. Alice carried James to all of his doctor and therapy appointments and through the contacts she made at the rehab hospital was able to get a good wheelchair at a very reduced price. Pushing James through her neighborhood, Alice learned of other handicapped children and offered support and encouragement to their families. During one visit I had with Alice I lamented how limited her life was for a young mother. Instead of feeling sorry for herself, Alice replied, "I am grateful for all of the people I have met as a result of James' condition. If James had been born normal I never would have met them." So, another valuable lesson that I learned that has stayed with me all these years.

❑

Charlotte Cook, a member of the lay missioner class of 1992, served in Africa until 2003. She lives in Wheaton, Md., near one of her favorite cities, Washington, D.C. She works for IT Shows, Inc., as assistant director of a contract with U.S. Agency for International Development, where she supervises about 100 staff and carries out HR duties and general administrative tasks. Charlotte enjoys gardening, reading, cooking, and walking. She volunteers with the American Councils for International Education. Her team evaluates applications from high school students in former Soviet Union countries and the Balkans who want to spend a year in the United States. She escorts students back home when their year is complete. This year she will be accompanying students returning to Macedonia.

Dick Ramsay, Priest and Prophet

Frank Gerace ('64)

DICK RAMSAY WAS ASSIGNED TO BOLIVIA in 1964. From the day of his arrival to the then small town of Montero, he was beloved by the economically and emotionally powerless.

He spent most of his time listening to and counseling the sick and discouraged. He was loved always by many, but he became hated by others when in September 1969 he wrote a letter to the parish criticizing the upcoming agricultural fair. He pointed out the waste and socioeconomic and ecological consequences of the crops, fertilizers, and equipment that were touted by the importers and fledgling agro-businesses.

Few understood his firm stand against the Fair. Most of the middle class and clergy were prone to oracular statements about the pros and cons of the rapid extension of agricultural capitalism. Ramsay unequivocally based his stand on the statements of the Latin American bishops who the year before in Medellín, Colombia, had called attention to the reality of "internal colonialism." He wrote: "The Fair shows off the progress of a small group of people...reality is not shown in the Fair; the shacks of the people living on unpaved streets, their coughs and tuberculosis, hunger and poverty. This is not shown in the Fair....My brothers, poor farmers and workers, I have to tell you to not expect anything from the Fair because the Fair doesn't offer you anything. Don't be deceived by its glossiness nor by its disoriented 'development.'"

He was back a year later, in September of 1970, when he actively led protests at the actual fairgrounds. In October he refused to bless a new sawmill. He would not look back in his rejection of unbridled "development." Nor would his critics look back to the gentle Padre Ricardo of before.

Time has proven him to be a prophet. Santa Cruz, the sleepy traditional city where rich and poor shared a common culture, is now a glittering cross between Los Angeles and Rio de Janeiro.

The Fair *did* accompany "development," development rife with stark divides in levels of wealth, health, and opportunities. Imports soared. Gated neighborhoods with armed guards surrounded by enormous "marginal neighborhoods" began to ring the city.

The Fair *did* teach. It taught all that their previous frugality and restraint were backward. They learned that development and modernity demanded borrowing to have the latest consumer goods. The poor also learned well the lessons of their "betters." They learned to reach for what others have, even if it demanded levels of violence never seen before.

Dick was the bellwether, the cultural whistle-blower who saw the intent of "agricultural development" years before it became clear that free trade policies would ruin the already impoverished farmers of Africa, Haiti, Mexico, and elsewhere. He didn't know

Farmhouse, Maryknoll Novitiate, Hingham, Massachusetts

about Monsanto and its "patented" seeds. He didn't know about policies in the United States that give subsidies for inefficient and superfluous ethanol production. He couldn't foresee that agricultural land all over the globe would be bought up and taken out of the hands of the small farmer to be used for more profitable biofuel.

But he must have felt it all coming. In a short while, the lands to the north of Montero that had been cleared by small homesteaders were bought up and consolidated into huge tracts of Japanese and Brazilian soy farms. The Fair helped agro-business be more efficient in their sending the poor farmer to the slums of Santa Cruz.

Dick was not a Luddite. He was not against technological progress. He was not an economist; he was a pastor. He tried to warn Santa Cruz that any "development" that increased inequality was immoral. If there had been those with ears who could hear, they might have worked with him to teach and learn what true human development could be.

However, no one heard. Some of his strongest critics were members of Maryknoll. This is not the place to try to identify their motives. We only have the evidence of the letters of disavowal of Ramsay that they sent to the press.

Dick belongs with prophets like Luigi Sturzo, Danilo Dolci, and César Chávez, who have fought for justice in the fields. They did not prevail neither did the Old Testament prophets, but their word and example still challenge our complacent consciences.

❑

Frank and Miriam Gerace live in La Gran Manzana, New York. Look them up for good Italian and Bolivian food and an ample supply of glassware for whatever you bring on your visit. They have five children and six grandchildren. They both still work part-time, which cuts into the time they would like to spend fighting corporate subversion of democracy at home and U.S. imperialism abroad. They have lost interest in much of the Vatican except for the architecture, art, and food.

Transformation:
A Cultural Odyssey

Paul Newpower ('69)

MY FIRST IMPRESSION OF MARYKNOLL was a picture in the *Maryknoll* magazine of a priest standing behind a group of Japanese children eating watermelons. I thought, I could be that guy, hanging out with those beautiful children somewhere in the Orient.

Glen Ellen had just doubled the size of the seminary in 1962, when I arrived, to accommodate 600 young seminarians. It was an amazing group of idealistic, tough, friendly, intelligent young men, and being a part of them excited me tremendously. We all shared the same dream of going to some far-off country as missionaries. Those were formative years for a young man just out of St. Paul, Minn., with hardly a clue as to what was happening in the world.

We were privileged to be studying theology shortly after the Second Vatican Council. Seminary training whetted my appetite for social activism and for a deeper spirituality. Life-long celibacy did not sound great to me at the time, but, heck, maybe the pope would change that rule in the not-too-distant future. Nor did I feel comfortable with the clericalism that separated us from the general life of the laity. But priesthood in Maryknoll was the way to be a missionary, and that's what I wanted most of all.

In our deacon year we were surprised to find that our rector, Fr. George Weber, had left the priesthood to marry a former nun. It was the start of the exodus from the priesthood. Twenty of us were ordained to the priesthood in 1969. Full of enthusiasm for adventure I wanted to follow the advice of Dorothy Day who said, "The best thing to do with the best things you have is to give them away."

There had developed in me a sense of restlessness, not wanting to settle down to a monotonous sort of life. I wanted to leave behind my previous life and embark on a journey into the unknown, to go to a faraway place, and hopefully, on the journey, to discover new aspects of my own deeper self and the face of God. I felt I wanted to let go of what seemed most clear, most secure in the hope of finding something more profound, more meaningful, more worthwhile. I remembered the words of St. Augustine, "My heart is restless until it rests with you, my God."

There was also a desire to put myself into a situation where I would be confronted with others who were vastly different from me, to learn from them how they viewed the world and God. And hopefully to share in some way with their struggles for a better world. I wanted to go to Latin America because it seemed a revolutionary place. The General Council chose Bolivia for me as my destiny. Seemed like a good mission place to go. I thought if Jesus were to return, he would probably choose a country like Bolivia, so similar to Palestine at the time, poor, insignificant, and at the margin of the Roman Empire. Unlike Jesus, I still held on to some pretensions of wanting to change the world, or at least the Church, or maybe something of Bolivia.

Shortly after my arrival in Bolivia, two of the Maryknoll superiors in Bolivia left to get married, and a couple of years later one of the priests who arrived with me left and married a local Bolivian woman. Had the thought crossed my mind? Sure! Bolivian women were quite friendly to us new missionaries, eager to speak some Spanish, to get to know the culture, and explore our new surroundings. The fact that we were priests seemed to give them a sense of security that we were not on the make. Meanwhile, we were struggling with culture shock. The frustration of not being able to communicate and feelings of inadequacy about how to act in society produced a sense of insecurity and alienation. We were good targets for a sweet Bolivian woman to hold our hands and reassure us that everything was all right.

After a year in La Paz I asked to be assigned to Achacachi, a rural church in the midst of the Aymara culture. I felt I had really arrived in mission, in a vastly different, non-Western culture. My enthusiasm dwindled when, several months later, the priest with whom I had been working left for the States on vacation and never came back. I ended up alone in Achacachi.

Those were lonely times. I liked the adventure of immersing myself in the Andean Indian culture. But I was always an outsider. It takes a long time to become a friend of the Aymara people. They are suspicious of outsiders and only after months or years of respectful friendship does one gain their confidence. During the days I was on the road with my motorcycle to visit one of the 65 rural villages and our religious leaders. But back home I would huddle alone around my kerosene stove to keep warm. This lonely existence was not my cup of tea.

I wondered whether anyone cared that I was in Achacachi. What difference did it make that I was out there on a lonely mission post in the middle of nowhere, struggling to keep warm and to keep my spirits up? I thought of so many others in comfortable surroundings with friends close at hand.

One day I drove my motorcycle up through the mountains. I drove off the road close to the 17,000-foot permanent snow line, parking as close as I could get to the sheer steepness of majestic Mount Illampu, rising 6,000 feet almost straight up in front of me. Looking across the deep chasm that separated us, I felt so small, insignificant, and vulnerable. No one was there but me and the spirits of the mountain. I shivered as the cold wind howled around me and felt overwhelmed by the immense mountain in front of me. It was desolate and bleak and I became frightened. I felt an urge to leap.

What was that urge to destruction? I felt like Christ being tempted in the desert, alone and facing terror. I had wanted to come to this edge to test myself, to test the Lord, to face God alone and without all the security I usually guarded myself with. I prayed a desperate prayer and slowly backed away from the edge. Trembling, I mounted my motorcycle and retreated from the temptation of that awful beauty.

Rather desperately, I talked with some fellow Maryknollers in the neighboring churches of Peñas and Huarina who also were alone. We decided to form a team, live in one central place, and from there serve the other churches. At last I had some company and some people to share my life with.

But as time wore on, I wore out. After six years in Achacachi, I began to lose my enthusiasm for this great mission adventure. I was getting cranky and short-tempered with the people and wondered if maybe I was doing more harm than good by staying there. I talked with my religious superiors and they suggested I return to the States for a while and work in promotion. But I felt like I was giving up the ship, abandoning my mission work and my people. I looked around at the other Maryknollers who had been in Bolivia for 20 or 30 years and were still at their posts. I bet they came down to Bolivia like me with a lot of piss and vinegar, all enthusiastic about serving the Lord and the people. But then, after many years of loneliness and frustrations, trying to give themselves to the people, and getting so little back, they burned out. But they stayed at their posts. They came down to Bolivia as missionaries to give their lives to the people, and they would die with their boots on. They would not admit defeat or throw in the towel. But often they became bitter, resentful, lonely old men. A few thrived and maintained a lively, loving, open spirit. But they were few and far between.

I guess I had given Achacachi my best shot and some of the best years of my life. So in the end I decided to finish this phase of my mission career and go back to the States for a while. Who knows? Maybe those feelings of worthlessness, of purposelessness, of futility, would pass by some day, and not last forever. Maybe I could recover my enthusiasm. Maybe even come back to Bolivia.

Returning home to St. Paul, I began to realize that I had left home by one door and had returned through another. It was not the same place anymore. And I was not the same person who had left St. Paul 15 years earlier. Too much had happened, too many jolting experiences. Home was no longer familiar to me. I felt out of place and began to realize how much I was still living out of the radically different experiences I had had in Bolivia among the Aymara Indians. It came out in an irritability I felt toward people around me who didn't seem concerned or sensitive to all the anguish I was feeling for the people in Latin America.

After a couple of years in Minneapolis, and several at Maryknoll, N.Y., in the Media Relations Office, I began to feel again that maybe I had bitten off more than I could chew. I guessed life had been a little too hectic and intense for me over the years, and I needed some time to step back and see where I was. Maryknoll was extremely generous in giving me a long break for some needed physical and personal recovery time. The dark side, my shadow side, with all my failings, had always been an enigma to me. I knew I wasn't perfect, that I had my faults, my sins. Sometimes I even felt an inclination to flirt with that, which I knew was wrong, a disturbing tendency to evil, which really scared me. The dilemma of St. Paul encouraged me. He wrote: "I begged the Lord three times to take it away, but He responded: My strength is sufficient for you, for my strength is made manifest in your weakness."

With some help I also began to realize that I was living outside of myself, living on the expectations of others, trying too hard to perform for them. I was overly concerned about my image and was losing touch with my own emotions and needs. Thanks be to God and the support of so many good people around me who drew me along and gently lifted me back into a more healthy state of mind, body, soul, and spirit. But I still wondered about my future, Some people counseled me to stay in the States and even seek some other options in life. But something had a hold on me to return to Bolivia. I believe it was the radically different lifestyle and values there that attracted me, a slower pace of life, less aggressive, more homey and friendly. Even God seemed more real to me there. The

Aymara Indian village in Achacachi, Bolivia

149

only problem was the anguish I always felt in my soul for the undeserved suffering of so many innocent people. Mission was in my soul. So with Maryknoll's blessing it was back to Bolivia again.

In 1990 many of the Maryknoll priests in Bolivia were older now, had borne the heat of long missionary careers, and were less enthusiastic about the great missionary adventure of Maryknoll. I was at a different point in my life and hoped I could still energetically embrace a new beginning to my missionary vocation.

In Cochabamba, Fr. Tom McBride suggested I work in a far corner of his parish that was largely unattended. He told me that two young lay missionary women had recently moved into the area, and the support of a priest would be very helpful to them. With that suggestion, Tom unwittingly opened a door to my future destiny. Rebeca was one of the two young pastoral workers there. And so, Rebeca and I became companions in ministry.

When my six-year assignment came to an end, I was faced with what to do next. The Maryknoll General Council had published a document in 1995 called "Journeying in Hope and Trust." The document stated

> "The context of mission today offers radically different challenges that call for creativity, integrity and authenticity. Tried and true methods may no longer suffice.... New paradigms are still to be born.... Each of us appropriates the Maryknoll spirit in new and creative ways, not without tensions and misunderstandings, but with the firm conviction that this is the direction the Spirit is calling us to take.... One can no longer be content to remain with what existed before.... Everyone is called to venture beyond their safe space.... The first journey in mission is merely a preparation for the second.... Embracing these values invites not only persecution and risk, ambiguity and uncertainty, but also an infinite amount of new opportunities and creativity to search for and discover Christ among all of God's peoples."

Those words actually inspired me with the courage and trust to consider a dramatic change in my life in mission.

I certainly wasn't getting any younger, and if I had any inkling of moving on from the priesthood and starting a new lifestyle, then I'd better not wait too long. Rebeca and I had become close over the years and we shared many values in our faith, in our commitment to the poor, in the cultural realities of Bolivia, in seeking a simple lifestyle in prayer and solidarity with those in need. We had struggled through a lot of ambiguity in our relationship but in the end, we realized we really cared for one another. I seriously considered for the first time in my life the real possibility of leaving the priesthood and getting married. Nothing is forever. I prayed about it, and talked it over with my family and with some friends whom I thought would understand. The more we talked, the more that direction seemed right for me at that time in my life. And the more it seemed that God was calling me in that direction for a new mission paradigm.

Finally one day I spoke to Rebeca. I guess I asked her if we might consider getting together, you know, like joining together as a couple, maybe getting married.... I guess I proposed! It would mean that we would not separate now, that we would continue and deepen our relationship into the future, that our ministries would now move in new directions. We talked and talked about the possibility. We realized we loved one another and it seemed right for us to take this dramatic step into the unknown. It seemed that God was with us and leading us down an uncharted pathway. And it was a call we did not want to miss, no matter the risks involved. Our hearts felt good about it, and we both said yes. We worried about getting a job, about supporting ourselves, about where we would live, about what our friends would say, about staying in Bolivia. But in spite of it all, we wanted to take the step and make the commitment to one another, trusting that God would see us through the difficulties. With that confirmation full of ambiguity, I finally spoke to one of the Maryknoll superiors. He was understanding but asked me to return to the States for consultation.

At Maryknoll, N.Y., I requested a leave of absence. My superiors wanted me to leave Bolivia for a year to decide what I wanted to do with my life. But in no way was I interested in leaving Rebeca nor Bolivia. We had already decided! I didn't need any more time for discernment. But I agreed to step back from my ministry and the priesthood and Maryknoll and explore life outside the fold of religious life, in Bolivia. In my diary I wrote: "I pray, Loving Spirit, your sacred help and sustenance for this mysterious venture that I am so reluctant to embrace, yet so anxious to realize."

Before getting married, Rebeca and I went around together in Cochabamba and told people that we were planning to get married. Some were very supportive, but others were actually quite shocked and dismayed; some even consulted with a priest who told them not to associate with us. Rebeca was worried that people would blame her for stealing a priest away from his vows; at least that was a common notion in Bolivia. But Bolivia has few celibate priests. Many local priests have a close woman friend and children, putting up a front that the woman is a relative or housekeeper, without making any formal declaration of marriage. People know. The bishops know. And they all look the other way. It is hypocrisy, but it serves to maintain the functional role of priesthood in society.

Rebeca and I married in a civil ceremony on January 27. I was, of course, nervous. But also really excited about beginning this new phase of my life. It was something I had always had in the back of my mind, to live a normal life, be a normal person, with no pretensions, to join the human race in all its struggles and joys. This seemed like a very good way to become acculturated into the Bolivian mainstream, to become as much as possible a part of them.

A few years later our first child was born. We named him Elias in memory of Rebeca's dear brother who had been killed in an automobile accident. Three years later Rosie came along. We named after my spunky 91-year-old mother in St. Paul. Here I was, the father of two little children at 63 years of age. Life just unfolds that way. I have no regrets. I thoroughly enjoyed my 25 years as a Maryknoll missionary priest. And I am thoroughly enjoying my years now as a regular family man. It is just what was missing in my life. Not a minute available now to be lonely. The house is full of laughter and children quarreling and all the little daily routine activities that keep one so busy.

So many of my previous anxieties have diminished, only to be replaced by others of a more domestic kind . But now I have a partner to share them with, and two lovely children who yank me back to this reality with their needs for affection and reassurance. I never used to worry about anything, even death. But now life seems so much more precious to me and for my family. I worry now for what sometimes seems a precarious future. I only pray for confidence that God will see us through anything that may come our way.

And here I am, an immigrant as my ancestors had been, still journeying in a strange land. I yearn to belong here, to fit into the culture and be accepted and appreciated, to feel that I matter to others around me, that I am worthwhile and can contribute something to my surroundings. I long to blend in and not have people ask me where I am from. But my accent betrays me and people often initially speak loudly to me, thinking that will help me understand what they are saying. My looks also betray me and I stand out like a sore thumb among all the dark Latin and Indian people of Bolivia. For as hard as I try, I am still an outsider in Bolivia and my roots are still in the States. One does not leave that heritage behind. I have a foot in both cultures and can never escape the ambiguity of not really belonging here nor probably belonging any more, I suspect, back in the States.

My missionary witness? It seems it now blends in with a rather normal life. My faith witness is now as a family. We struggle along with other people to make ends meet. We suffer many of the same hardships of health and security and adequate income. We share with others in a trust that God will provide. Rebeca still shares her ministry as a social worker. Hopefully our faith in a loving God shines through and even brightens up the lives and struggles of others. And hopefully our lives and our resources shared with others in this little corner of the world might in some small way contribute to the unfolding of the reign of God.

❑

Paul, Rebeca, and the children live in Cochabamba, Bolivia. He can be reached via email at pnewpower@hotmail.com.

Roots and Wings

Kevin Reid ('71)

I JOINED MARYKNOLL IN SEPTEMBER 1964, a magical
time for the church, and for our country, as it was the early part
of the great sixties revolutions about civil rights, the war, and personal freedom. It was a heady time. I remember being pretty
nervous when I first arrived at Glen Ellyn. My trip there was the
first time I had ever been on an airplane, and the first time I had
ever lived away from home, even though I entered Glen Ellyn as a
junior, after two years at Boston College. I was a day student at
BC, and I had never been away to summer camp or any other place,
so GE for me was my first experience living apart from my parents.
I was homesick at first, but that quickly changed as I settled into
the seminary schedule and started to make friends with my classmates. My principle recollection of the GE experience is what a
great group of people were there. That included the teachers, my
classmates, and the rest of the students from the other classes. It
was the most collegial time of my life. We were bonded by a common aspiration, to be a missioner, and the spirit was one for all and
all for one. Everyone was so willing to help each other. No one was
trying to be better than the rest. Whenever I had a problem, needed
help with an assignment, or just needed someone to listen, someone was always there, just as I tried to be there for anyone who
needed me. I really learned the true meaning of friendship and in-
terdependence during my seminary days. It is the most lasting
memory of my Maryknoll experience and the most profound. It
helped make me the person I have become, and I'm forever grateful for it.

After I left Maryknoll in 1967, I didn't really know what I

Maryknoll College, Glen Ellyn, Illinois

wanted to do. I entered the business world, got into human resources work and spent most of my career as an HR manager for a
high-tech company based in Massachusetts. I eventually got into
the international side of HR work, and I spent the last 20 years of
my career traveling all over the world. I had originally wanted to
spend my life overseas as missioner, and I think it was that spirit of
adventure, which was instilled in me during my days at Glen Ellyn,
that led me to work internationally. I believe that the things I
started learning about other countries and cultures during my seminary days helped me to be more appreciative of the people that I
worked closely with many years later in places such as Malaysia,
Singapore, Shanghai, Korea, and Japan, as well as less exotic
places like Paris, London, and Puerto Rico. My joy in traveling and
my desire to learn about other cultures started with Maryknoll, and
I believe the training that I got in my seminary days has made me a
better person in my working life, from an ethical, moral, and
intercultural viewpoint.

My Maryknoll experience has also helped to shape my personal
and family life. My wife and I tried to instill a spirit of adventure in
our two daughters, and both of them have spent significant time
living in and learning about other cultures. Our elder daughter,
Carole, is multilingual, having spent a year in high school as an ex-

155

change student in France. She then majored in Russian in college, spent a semester living with a Russian family in St. Petersburg shortly after the collapse of the Soviet Union, and now lives with her husband and two children in Hong Kong, where she is working to master Mandarin. Our younger daughter, Colleen, lived in Spain for a year in high school, and spent a semester in college living with a family in Venezuela. I like to think that I was able in some way to pass on to them some of the values of respecting and honoring people in other cultures and countries that I learned in my seminary days.

I am now retired and spending a lot of time doing volunteer work in the Boston area, and loving it. One of my volunteer activities is working at St. Francis House, a shelter in downtown Boston where I work one day a week with two of my classmates, Doc Miller and Ed Rogers. We provide clothing to the homeless on Friday mornings, and then have coffee together, where we solve all the world's problems, and do a fair amount of reminiscing about our years together at Glen Ellyn.

It's been quite a journey, both literally and figuratively, since I first stepped on that airplane and flew to Glen Ellyn. I've enjoyed the ride, and hope to continue the ride for a while longer.

❑

Kevin Reid ('71) and his wife Terrie are retired and living in Andover, Mass. They are both active in volunteer activities in their community, and they spend a lot time of time traveling, mostly to visit their two daughters. Carole lives in Hong Kong with her husband and two children, and Colleen lives in San Francisco with her husband.

For Joe Carney ('65)

Joseph Hart Patrick Carney's family, Suga, Mark F., and Hana Marion Carney

IN HONOR OF JOSEPH PATRICK CARNEY, we, his family, would like to send their heartfelt congratulations on the 100th anniversary of the founding of the Maryknoll Mission Society of Fathers and Brothers. Maryknoll played a significant role in Joe's life. We send our deepest respect, love, and gratitude to Maryknoll.

Over the years, Maryknoll gave Joe a multitude of opportunities to learn and deepen his understanding of the world and the loving relationship between God and people. Maryknoll provided Joe an outlet for his compassionate nature and afforded him the opportunity to experience cultures around the world, while serving its people in mission.

Joe joined Maryknoll after graduating from the College of the Holy Cross, the Jesuit liberal arts school in Worcester, Mass. Upon ordination, Joe received his Maryknoll assignment to teach college seminarians in Glen Ellyn, Ill., Los Altos, Calif., and Scranton, Pa.; and then he was appointed vice rector of Maryknoll's major seminary in New York. Finally, after gaining his PhD in African Studies from St. John's University, Joe received an overseas assignment to Tanzania in East Africa. He served two years in Nieghina by Lake Victoria after completing Swahili language study. He often shared fond memories of life in Africa.

After leaving Maryknoll and receiving a dispensation from the Vatican in 1976, Joe established an adult education program with the College of New Rochelle in the South Bronx. He began the evening program with 12 students in the basement of a Catholic church. Two years later, working with Christian Brothers, he developed the program to more than 700 students. In 1978, he took a job with USAID and began his 33-year career in the U.S. Foreign Service.

His first USAID assignment was as an education and development officer to Lethoso, the mountainous, independent nation completely surrounded by South Africa. Joe continued his foreign service in Tanzania, Indonesia, and Jamaica. One of his proudest accomplishments was the implementation of a locally developed "Free Textbook to All" program in Jamaica in 1983. He presented

Mother and children, Ghana

his ideas to five major donor countries and partnered with a major local newspaper to produce Jamaica's own school textbooks, a solution to the expensive prices students had to pay for books imported from England. This effort was culturally significant and allowed students to take pride in their own culture and history,

Back in Washington, D.C., Joe served in the State Department's Office of Overseas Schools, then again in USAID as the director of its Worldwide Education Department. He tirelessly represented the U.S. government in Unesco, especially in the Education for All Fast Track Initiative (FTI). The FTI program invites and organizes bilateral and multilateral donors to provide primary-level education for the young and not so young. Throughout his government career he never lost his dedication for projects big or small, which often provided a voice to people in developing nations who needed it most.

He spent his life providing basic education and development opportunities for the underprivileged people of the world. Wherever he was, he always looked for opportunities to assist Maryknoll missionaries. The life lessons taught by Maryknoll gave Joe the strength and determination to persevere through difficult situations, while still forming sincere relationships with everyone he encountered. He was a man who followed Maryknoll's vision. To this day our family receives gracious calls from people whose lives he enriched.

From the above, you can tell how proud we are of Joe's dedicated life not only for our family but also for God's needy people at home and abroad. We are forever grateful for the immense opportunities and blessings that Maryknoll Fathers and Brothers provided for Joe. Congratulations to Maryknoll for producing fine, dedicated men to serve God and the world throughout the past 100 years—and our sincerest hopes for many more years in the future.

❏

Suga Carney and family, 13208 Coralberry Dr., Fairfax VA 22033-1505.

A Compelling Presence

Paul Segall ('59)

MY PARENTS HAD 14 CHILDREN. I'm the oldest. The evening of one day when I was 12 years old and there were 7 children, my father was trying to persuade my mother to get out of the house to go to the movies. "You've been working all day," he said. "You need some diversion." "But I still have a pile of ironing to do," my mother replied, pointing to a pile of clothes stacked on the kitchen table. "Let it wait," my father said. And so, after putting my five brothers and one sister to bed, they left me in charge and left for the movies.

I finished some homework and suddenly got a bright idea, an inspiration, that I felt had to be followed: I would iron that pile of clothes. And so I did. When my parents came back and saw the clothes all ironed, they were pleased and happy. But what I mostly remember was the compelling Presence and joy that ironing those clothes brought me.

On another day, when I was 14 and had 6 brothers and 1 sister, I got another bright idea, an inspiration: I would do the supper dishes; my mother could sit down and rest. And from that day till I left for the army in 1945 I always did the dishes after supper. And here again what I remember most was the compelling Presence and joy washing the dishes brought to me.

After finishing pre-med in Catholic University in 1951 I was accepted at Marquette School of Medicine but had to delay going there for two years because my father had become very sick and someone had to support our family of 12. I remember at that time working as an electrician and again experiencing that compelling Presence that made the work a joy.

In 1953, after my father had recovered, I did enter Marquette School of Medicine and was doing quite well. One day, however, I went over to the anatomy lab to review for an exam, and since we did not have classes on Saturday, it was quiet, and when I took a break from my review, I again felt a compelling Presence and joy that said I should become a priest. A few days later I discussed this with my spiritual director and he suggested I wait a little. But I saw no point in waiting because I was so sure. I visited the Maryknoll College at Glen Ellyn, not far from Marquette, and they recommended that I transfer to the Liberal Arts College at Marquette, taking a few courses in philosophy and Latin, go to the Venard in the summer, and then back to Glen Ellyn in the fall. This I did and have never regretted it. I was 27 years old.

I spent six happy years at Glen Ellyn, Bedford, and Maryknoll; and then ten happy years on the mission in Korea.

However, one day in 1969, while I was walking meditatively to a mission station, the same Presence again inspired me—this time to leave Maryknoll. It seemed quite negative—not like ironing clothes, washing dishes, or supporting a family.

But what was I leaving for, I asked myself? Yet, I trusted that in time I would find out. However, of this I was sure: the urge to leave Maryknoll was just as compelling as the inspiration to enter Maryknoll.

A few days later I informed Bishop Pardy and then the regional superior, Dan Schneider, of my decision and started the process for laicization, which went very smoothly.

My father and I were very close and when he died in March of 1965, I was pastor of a church here in Korea and since at that time Maryknoll policy did not allow anyone to return to the States until he was six years on the mission, I said a High Requiem Mass for him here in Korea. What was significant was that I in no way grieved to say the mass without my family back in the United States. The reason is that from that moment hardly a day goes by that I don't feel my dad's presence and often ask a favor.

This was also true when my mother, three of my brothers, and three of my sisters passed on: I become aware of their presence in God and frequently seek their help. Jesus said, "It is good for you that I go." And that when he went, he would send the Spirit and who we are and what we are is largely determined by how we respond to the Spirit. Outside of my own family, I have found that not a few Maryknollers, especially those that were here on the mission with me in Korea, have helped me after they passed on and are now with the Lord and still dedicated to this mission as I am.

And so I have stayed on here in Korea, have taught English in several Korean universities, and am now retired. I live alone with my Korean wife. We have two children, both of whom married and have returned to the States.

I visit the Maryknoll Center House in Seoul three or four times a year, have a meal with the men, and pick up some good books. Karl Rahner said that a vocation should be open-ended. Right now I'm a "monk on the missions." It's a happy life. I'm 84.

❏

Paul Segall, Samho Apt 15-1101, Anyang, Pisandong 341, 431-737 South Korea.

Forever in My Dreams

Lawrence D. Obrist ('69)

EVEN THOUGH MORE THAN 50 YEARS HAVE PASSED since I entered Glen Ellyn in September 1960, anywhere from five to six times a year I still find myself reliving some aspect of Maryknoll in my dreams. Often it is bits or pieces of life from Glen Ellyn, Hingham, or the Knoll, certain classmates, a merging with Army life, or just a pure symbolic amalgam. Reflecting on this pattern, it struck me as odd, but to be an accepted fact of life, that being an alumnus of the Class of 1969 and nearly seven years in Maryknoll influenced my life.

It all began long ago and far away on a planet called Nebraska, or "flat water," a name the Otoe tribe gave to the Platte River. In June 1960, when my father called me away from lawn mowing to tell me that a priest was at our home wanting to talk with me, I know he was pleasantly surprised that I was even considering a vocation. Fr. Peter Byrne had come all the way from Denver, 500 miles away. Next thing I knew I was on a train to Denver for the psychological screening by Fr. Paul D'Arcy.

I was always envious of classmates who could relate their colorful and inspiring stories of introductions to Maryknoll and decisions to join. To this day, I don't know what magazine coupon I filled out to bring Fr. Byrne to my door. I barely had heard of the SVD (Divine Word) Fathers or the Columban Fathers based in Omaha. I can only guess that it might have been an ad in one of the Catholic magazines to which my parents, Charles and Agnes, subscribed. I had not yet laid my eyes on the *Maryknoll* magazine.

My uncle, Msgr. Lawrence F. Obrist, was disappointed that I did not consider the Diocese of Lincoln, but he spoke highly of a classmate, Fr. Edward Weis. He remembered well a Maryknoll priest speaking to his class at St. Francis Major Seminary in Milwaukee. He managed to steal Ed Weis away to join the burgeoning missionary group. My uncle's diary for May 29, 1929, related: "By the way, a young Maryknoll Father spoke here last night, Fr. John M. Martin. He is a Milwaukee boy. The society is that of American missionaries that was founded 18 years ago to train priests for the missions."

Maryknoll's recruitment harvest from Nebraska has always been sparse. Older priests recalled Fr. Raymond Hohlfeld among the old China hands. Research revealed Frs. J. Patrick McMahon and James W. O'Neill in the 1955 ordination class. In 1966, I met the only Nebraska Maryknoll Brother, Marvin Mayberger. In 2002, Fr. Steve DeMott rescued my Peace Corps son, Brian, who was then passing through Lima, Peru.

Freshman year at Glen Ellyn found me thrown in with the "seminary pros" of the Boston Latin and Venard variety and a few others in all classes who considered themselves among the Eastern "elite." Freshman year anywhere is stressful and challenging for one to fit in and keep up with classes. The high school of my hometown of Steinauer, population 120, did not have the language courses and caliber of other classes to match what I found at G.E. Frs. John McCormack, Tom Wilcox, and Bart Galvin thankfully were patient with my Latin ability over the years, as Fr. Greg Keegan also was with my sophomore Spanish. My language gene finally bloomed with sons Brian and Pat's Peace Corps Spanish and French.

Frs. John McConnell and Bill Frazier opened my eyes to the method and message of the Scripture and Fr. Bill Coleman to economics. Fr. George Buckley challenged me with logic, and Fr. George Pfister helped me limp through his math elective. Fr. Jack Halbert tried to help me find the message and symbolism in poetry, and Fr. Charles Cappel helped unravel the mystery of biology and identify the evil of the birth control pills that we came across sorting medicines for the missions. I think of Fr. Arthur Merfeld's meal-reading training every time I am lector at our Cathedral of the Risen Christ. Up to his untimely death in August of 1962, we knew what "fear of the Lord" was by looking into the stern face of Fr. Norbert Fleckenstine when confessing our violations of some part of the Rule. The Fifth Amendment was of no value in front of him.

As the only Husker in our class, I was supposed to fit the farm-boy stereotype. But I considered myself a "town kid." I never did live on a farm, but I learned what hard, hot, and dirty work was by working on them. My Swiss great-grandfather, Joseph Steinauer, founded our town in 1856, and it was named after him. On my mother's side, my roots were with the pre–Civil War Irish in Boston's North End, and East Boston's Holy Redeemer and Star of the Sea churches. My great-grandfather, Patrick Barry, was a Civil War amputee vet.

At 18, I was too young to vote in JFK's election win of 1960, but I found many other liberal students who enlarged and helped form my political views. Maryknoll mission locations enlarged my worldview and I discovered, sadly, how many U.S. foreign policies made the lives of the poor worse.

I mastered the fine art of refined clerical swearing. The Glen Ellyn tradition had somehow generated the ubiquitous "crutch" as an expletive to cover all occasions. I embraced it with such gusto that I found myself glued to the moniker "Crutch."

During morning duties and manual labor, I had no trouble with the dish squad, "jake" detail, or trash run with Bob McClellan. A small perk of this was being allowed to drive a truck four blocks. One summer, I helped Brother Hilarian (William Flanagan) with the mail run to the post office in Glen Ellyn.

I now realize that early friendships were generated initially by the alphabet! This partially explained my warm and treasured friendship with Frs. Ray Nobiletti and Gerald O'Connor.

Even though I did not think I was deprived by growing up in a small town, Glen Ellyn introduced me to soccer, ice skating, tennis, and, almost in desperation, I tried handball!! Fr. Greg Keegan helped us order soccer shoes and ice skates. Fr. Tom ("Ho'o mali mali") Wilcox demonstrated the fine points of soccer. I celebrated my 21st birthday at Lake Geneva, Wisc., trying skiing for the first time with the coaching of Minnesota's Paul Newpower.

Sports were not my only initiation into a broader taste of the world. "Apostolic service" at Friendship House in Chicago offered me the opportunity to enter the home of a black family for the first time. St. Camillus Club took us to nursing homes to help reduce the loneliness and confusion of senior residents. The death of Fr.

John Kaserow's mother made me appreciate the additional 30 years I would enjoy with my mother.

My interest in photography advanced with the use of the darkroom and guidance of the many camera geeks. Tom Fenton and Ken Thesing put my skills to work with the *DuPage* newsletter.

Our 1960 class was one of the largest up to that time. Vocations seemed to be flooding in. This initiated the muck and mess of the construction expansion of Glen Ellyn. In the fall of 1962, we upperclassmen lived in pod groups and tasted fraternity life. I ended up with Phi Phi Tau group under Fr. Pfister, its name shortened to "Pfister's Twisters."

I was personally enthralled with the "talks" of Bishop Lane on China mission life in the thirties and the World War II years. Bishop John Comber or Vicar General Fr. John Donovan would occasionally visit and share some mission story or some points of inspiration for the sometimes cynical crowd, who thought they wanted to be missionaries. I had the pleasure of actually meeting a few of the pioneers, such as Fr. Tom Malone, Fr. Frederick Dietz, Fr. Bernard Meyer, and, naturally, my uncle's classmate of the Maryknoll Class of 1932, Fr. Edward Weis.

The fall of 1963 brought the tragedy of the assassination of President Kennedy. I still have the mark I made in my *Liber Usualis,* when we all went to the chapel for prayers on the Feast of St. Cecilia, November 22.

I had hoped using my 1959–ordained priest-brother Jack's copy of the *Summa Theologica* might give me an edge, but no such luck. With Fr. Frazier's patience and guidance, I managed the acceptance of my thesis on St. Thomas' fourth proof for the existence of God, the gradations of being. Fr. Buckley then capped off life in June of 1964, bestowing a BA degree, with my proud family looking on, along with a seminarian cousin, Larry Gyhra, who was ordained in 1966. I was glad for his presence, as I always felt treated as a traitor by some of the diocesan priests at home.

Our Class of 1969 opened the new novitiate at Hingham, Mass. This certainly was a year of bonding as a class and as Maryknoll under the tutelage of Fr. John McCormack, who was elected superior general by the time of our departure. I tested his flexibility by persuading him to allow me to return home just a week after arrival for the funeral of my 95-year-old grandfather. He picked me as his

Chapel, Maryknoll Novitiate, Hingham, Massachusetts

"office typing boy" during our novitiate. Teaching CCD to high school kids convinced me that education would not be my vocation.

By this year, we had a good idea of what real friendship that could last a lifetime was like. A sense of a Maryknoll family budded when spending our first Christmas away from home. Frs. Tom Cronin and James McNiff rounded out the novitiate staff for Fr. McCormack and they added their own mission-life perspective to our formation. The rocks tossed from the crowd during our march with the Catholic Interracial Council at the head of the 1965 St. Patrick's Day parade in South Boston reminded us that religion and racism can exist in the same hearts.

Church prayer life of the breviary and Liturgy of the Hours was initiated. It was a time to get comfortable in your skin with regular prayer and a personal spirituality. Your own vocation was tested as you witnessed classmates drop away, but it had more meaning as your first oath came at the end of novitiate.

Cardinal Cushing journeyed to Hingham for his first visit to the new novitiate and to preside over our First Oath. I was surprised and honored that my uncle, Msgr. Obrist, made the effort to be present. He ended up signing all our oaths as witness to the cardinal. Only now, I realize he had to accept that Maryknoll again stole away another vocation from him.

My time at the Knoll was from September 1965 to December

1966 through first and part of second theology. I was enthralled by Frs. Bill McCarthy in Church history, Larry Vaughn with Vatican II changes, and Joe Grassi in Scripture. We had the third- and fourth-year theology students to look up to as models as they slowly progressed toward ordination.

The Vietnam War continued to escalate. Draft card burning was frequent, and we learned that one of the first card burners from NYC was a former Maryknoll seminarian. One of the deacons had a brother in Vietnam who sent photos of some dead Vietcong, whom I thought I had to see to grasp what war was all about. A new man joined our class, who had been in the Army four years as an advisor in Vietnam. It was a chance to gather firsthand knowledge of what he did and saw from a personal and political perspective. Some West Point cadets came down for their retreats. We debated with them and among ourselves about the war and whether the United States could afford both "guns and butter," as a common slogan went. A similar debate grinds on today. We learned that some of the men who left had to face the draft and a high chance of going to Vietnam. Beside Fr. Vincent Capodanno, Mike F. Hendricksen and James R. Clifcorn are two others I know who lost their lives. Mike's picture is near the Maryknoll chapel and Jim is buried at the cemetery at Maryknoll. Later, one of our classmates, Don McDonough, made a major life decision as a CO (conscientious objector) and took on the consequences that changed the rest of his life.

Little did I realize that within a year I, too, would be caught in the military's web.

At the start of second theology, 1966, my vocational fervor began to wane. After a number of sessions with my spiritual director, one with Fr. Gene Kennedy, vocational testing, and a conference with the superior general, Fr. McCormack, I made the prayerful decision to depart from my path to the missionary priesthood through Maryknoll. Fortunately, then and now, I have been at peace with the decision.

My personal formation continued with three years in the Army, including 1968 in Vietnam as psych specialist with a med unit of the 25th Infantry Division at Cu Chi and Tay Ninh.

I heard that many others leaving Maryknoll had taken up some form of social work. Thus, the seed was planted for my social work graduate school of 1970–1972 at Loyola in Chicago. I returned to visit Glen Ellyn in 1971, and since my brother Jack lived in Glen Ellyn, I visited the old campus many times thereafter, only to see the original buildings, Fr. Norman Batt's additions and the chapel slide into vacancy, disrepair, and destruction. I took my last sad pictures in October 2006, when all was just flattened, green, park-district sod, with nothing left of Maryknoll but our 1964 flagpole in honor of President Kennedy.

Maryknoll's student address list could be used as a Rick Steves travel guide. I used it many times after leaving Maryknoll, especially when stationed at Natick, Mass., after returning from Vietnam. In 1969, I met my wife, Lorraine, through a party in Boston thrown by former classmate John Magnani. In May of 2004, son Pat and I arrived at the ultimate address in Rome, Via Sardegna, 83, the Maryknoll House. There we enjoyed the hospitality of the future superior general, Fr. Edward Dougherty!

I finally made it to the missions in February–March 2009, with son Patrick, who was working in Chad with Catholic Relief Services. Happily, I met classmate and former superior general, Fr. Ken Thesing, and others at the Maryknoll House in Nairobi, along with Fr. Dr. Bill Fryda at his St. Mary's Mission Hospital. In Mwanza, Tanzania, I attended Mass at a real mission parish, Transfiguration, in the Mabatina, arranged by Frs. David Smith and James Eble and Bro. Mark Huntington, who hosted us for lunch. In Dar es Salaam, Fr. John Waldrep managed to find our hotel and then an Italian restaurant in his Maryknoll pickup!

I am pained and disheartened by Maryknoll's vocation drought and its struggle for mission and facility operating funds. I can only help in my limited way with the latter. I know the Council leadership is struggling mightily for discernment to find creative ways to solve both problems.

Some may doubt that one religious institution could be so pivotal in the intellectual, emotional, cultural, physical, spiritual, and weltanschauung formation of one soul. But for me, I find myself still rehashing those events in my dreams in hopes of finding meaning and maybe a better ending.

❑

Lawrence and his wife, Lorraine, live in Lincoln, Neb.

Primum Regnum Dei...
et Justicia Sua

Dan Maloney ('60)

BEFORE THERE WAS A NATIONAL PHENOMENON called the Tea Party, before there were Red States and Blue States, there were the "God Squad" and the "Mod Squad." This was the early 1970s and the place was the Maryknoll Society's Chile Region.

Salvador Allende was Chile's president and people of faith who supported his election to the presidency supported one another in the recently formed Christians for Socialism, who had recently met in international congress in Santiago. The Latin American bishops had met two years earlier in Medellín, Colombia, and applied the teachings of the Vatican Council to the reality of Latin America, in the process announcing a "preferential option for the poor" as integral to the Church's mission. The Allende government had recently completed the nationalization of the copper industry begun under the previous Christian Democratic government of Eduardo Frei. What alarmed the Nixon administration in Washington was the accompanying announcement by the Allende government that there would be no compensation for completing the nationalization due to excess profits that the Anacondas and Kennecotts of the copper world had expropriated from Chile during all the years of their exploitation of Chile's copper riches. If the Nixon administration were to allow the Allende government to claim excess profits in nationalizing Chile's copper industry, it was argued, no U.S. overseas investments anywhere would be safe from similar claims.

The Mod Squad in Chile rolled into action with open letters denouncing the efforts of Henry Kissinger to strangle the Allende government by suspending U.S. credit for Chile's trade with the United States. Other protests were directed at the machinations of Harold Geneen, the CEO of International Telephone and Telegraph (a major U.S. investor in Chile) and his plotting and funding of local efforts to organize anti-Allende opposition among American and Chilean executives.

The Mod Squad (a group of "young Turks" not unlike junior members of other Maryknoll mission groups) tangled with the God Squad principally in regional meetings where regional planning was discussed and policy changes were proposed. Both groups in Chile were small minorities with the vast majority of Maryknollers in the moderate center. The Mod Squad took its name from the TV series of the sixties and "God Squad" alliterated nicely. The God Squad were veteran Chile hands, some of them part of the original group sent to Chile after being repatriated from Korea post–Pearl Harbor. Before the local political scene heated up during the Allende years, this group had resisted the "new thinking" coming out of various readings of the recent Vatican Council. Regional meetings called to plan pastorally frequently bogged down in disagreements over fine points of theology and changes of emphasis in pastoral priorities.

I lay all this bit of history on the table as context for a journey that might be characterized as "coming of age," a typical process of growing up that any young person goes through, particularly after leaving the hothouse of academia and finding a niche in the work-a-day world. You start in your youth to learn about the world around you through things they teach you in school and new experiences that you have as you grow. Your idealism leads you to become critical of parents, teachers, leaders in government, and church. You want to do something to improve things, to make a difference. And before you know it, you are getting involved in action of one sort or another. You join a missionary group, the Peace Corps, the Papal Volunteers, Vista Volunteers. You become more aware politically. For me, the context in which this all occurred was provided by Maryknoll.

You may recognize the title I am giving to this memoir. This was the episcopal motto of Maryknoll's cofounder, James Anthony

Walsh. The phrase comes from Matthew 6:33, "Seek first the kingdom of God and his righteousness." A contemporary translation of this text (Marcus Borg) would have it: "Strive first for the kingdom of God and God's justice." From "righteousness" to "justice" expresses for me the journey I was on in Maryknoll.

Back in the seminary of the 1950s, justice, if talked about at all, referred to the social encyclicals of the popes, the right to a living family wage, the right to organize and bargain collectively, more Leo XIII and Pius XI than the Fair Labor Standards Act and the Wagner Act. Did this topic come up in ethics class at Glen Ellyn? I don't remember. I tend to think that social ethics took a back seat to personal ethics, like "De Sexto." Al Schwartz (who left Maryknoll because it was too "bourgeois" to become a SAMist and eventually incardinate in Pusan, Korea, and is now on a path to canonization) used to get a bulk order of the *Catholic Worker*. But reading about homelessness and the Bowery from Dorothy Day's perspective was a far remove from being there and mixing it up with residents and visitors. There may have been a reticence about clerical activism in the sociopolitical arena as a reaction to the extremism of the Father Coughlin era. Besides, the missioner's role precluded taking a public, critical stance on civil affairs in the host country. In any event, we were fighting a cold war with communism, and Maryknollers were taking it on the chin in Mao's China ("dry martyrs," Bishop Sheen called them). "Workers of the world, unite!" was our enemy's mantra, not ours.

Things got a little more down to earth the summer after second theology. A group of us went out to East Los Angeles to work with John Coffield in Dolores Mission. Later on, East L.A. would become much more of a conflict zone than it was then. And so too would John Coffield's status with Cardinal McIntyre, when John got called on the cardinal's carpet for his social activism. The most challenging experience for me that summer was a street preaching gig in Pershing Square in downtown L.A. that was all about apologetics, not any burning justice issue of the day.

Even when I spent the next summer studying Spanish in Ponce, Puerto Rico, in a program organized by Ivan Illich, the sociological input was more cultural than critical social analysis. Illich's right-hand man was a New York priest, Ted McCarrick, later to become cardinal archbishop of Washington, D.C., so justice issues were not yet so prominent on Illich's plate. A couple of years later Illich became persona non grata to the three bishops in Puerto Rico, when he openly supported Governor Munoz Marin's birth control policy. Thus was born Illich's operation in Cuernavaca, Mexico.

Scroll ahead to 1965. Maryknoll had sent me to do graduate study in counseling psychology. John XXIII had opened the Vatican Council, and the voting rights movement had begun to challenge the Jim Crow laws in the South. I had been teaching for nearly two years at Glen Ellyn, when John Comber, the superior general, came on visitation. He was concerned about how well I was adjusting to my work of teaching ethics and psychological screening of candidates. The fact that I was in personal therapy was concerning. He had a better prescription to offer. "What you need," he said with his jaw set firm and teeth almost clenched, "is to go to the missions." And, in spite of my mild protest to the contrary, he assigned me to Chile, a mission where he had worked briefly before becoming Super G.

It took me a few years to admit it, but he was right. What a grad school counseling practicum and a whole year's internship in the Catholic University counseling center had been unable to accomplish came to be in the grassroots of Chile—settling down to earth, getting out of my head, grappling with the gravely simple problems of poverty, scarcity and un- and under-employment, and working within the Chilean Church that had a highly developed social consciousness and had begun to initiate land reform on its large agricultural land holdings. The "missions" began the process of making me more socially aware and conscious of glaring systemic injustices.

I missed the first year of the Allende government while back in the States for 15 months of Clinical Pastoral Education (CPE). Maryknoll was implementing the Overseas Training Program (OTP) for its seminarians, and supervised field experience was the method for sifting valuable self-understanding from transcultural immersion and role exploration before final oath and ordination. CPE was the model of supervisor training chosen for OTP field supervisors, a role I had already assumed. CPE's intense focus on self-awareness in discerning the pastoral role and developing effectiveness in ministry was not explicitly directed to training for justice ministry, but it certainly opened the mental/emotional door to facing squarely the total reality of any person with whom you might be working as a missioner. The social dimension (in particular, Allende's Chile) would come to complement the individual focus of CPE's pastoral sensitization, in order to transform me into a member of the Mod Squad.

So, did Maryknoll make me into a member of the Mod Squad? Not really. But many Maryknollers did influence that outcome, even John Comber, in spite of his best intentions. How was he to know how events subsequent to 1965 would coalesce into a growing social awareness and passion for justice? The final session of Vatican II was still pending. The Latin American bishops were yet to meet in Medellín to apply conciliar teaching to the Latin continent. Allende was yet to come to power in Chile. Nixon and Kissinger were yet to team up and assert a distorted Monroe Doctrine once again in the twentieth Century. The OTP was yet to come out of the 1966 General Chapter. And so on....

Recently I met a Catholic woman who worked for the Conference of Catholic Bishops in Washington and had studied theology at Yale Divinity School in the 1980s. I asked her why she had gone to the seminary, expecting some reply about ordination. She said she did it to prepare herself for justice ministry. When I was in the seminary with Maryknoll, I would never have been able to articulate such a goal for myself. Maryknoll was a clerical society. The seminary was to prepare for the priesthood with a missionary specialization. But to do work for justice? In retrospect, there is no surprise here, given the times and the places in which all Maryknollers found themselves. Indeed, *Primum Regnum Dei...et justicia sua.*

❏

After 20 years of active membership in the Society's Education Department, Chile Region, and Office of Society Personnel, Dan resigned and moved to Chicago in 1980. He successfully transitioned into the field of human resource management, completed an MSIR degree at Loyola University, married Barbara Soricelli and partnered with her in raising two adopted sons, Michael and Marc. They have lived in Evanston, Ill., for the past 25 years, where they are active members of the St. Nicholas faith community. Through the years, Dan worked on the Joint Committee for a couple of terms and actively promoted his class's reunions.

Endangered Species

Al Stumph ('68)

WHERE HAVE ALL THE FLOWERS GONE?"** Pete Seeger's composition reached the height of its popularity among antiwar activists of the 1960s and 1970s, and now that first line runs through my mind when I recall my Maryknoll days. I'm prejudiced, but I think the Maryknoll Society blossomed most fully in the lives of the men ordained and professed during the 1950s, 1960s, and 1970s. Although the stories of the men from the Society's early decades inspired me to join them, it was the men of the 1950s, 1960s, and 1970s, my teachers and contemporaries, who caught the spirit of that era.

Among many others, I recall classmates Pat Hoffman, whose joy in everyday living put so much into perspective, and Miguel Aragon, whose personal integrity and determination set standards I still seek to attain today. The scholarship of teachers Bill McCarthy, Jack Casey, Gene Kennedy, to name only three among the many, taught me to think critically and to love questioning. I owe something of my success in life to every Maryknoller I encountered during my time with the Society, from my days at the Venard to my mission assignment in Hong Kong.

Our universe has always been a chaotic place. It started out with a Big Bang and ever since, its components have randomly been bumping into each other, destroying each other, and creating new wonders. Certainly the era during which I studied for the priesthood was filled with bumps and the promise of great things to come. We Maryknollers blossomed beautifully in the chaos of the 60s and the years following, whether within the Society or on other paths. But now we are aging, and in the same way of every generation before us, we are an endangered species. We march inexorably toward extinction.

Eventually historians will look back at us and write definitive histories of the 1960s and 70s. To make sense of our times they will place our stories and lives in orderly rows and columns. In an effort to make their task easier, I'll write a little of my story here.

I entered the Venard as a high school freshman in 1955, was ordained in 1968, and resigned from Maryknoll and my priesthood eighteen months later. The realities of adolescence and young adulthood encompass my Maryknoll memories. I remember best my theology years. The grades on my transcript clearly reflect what classes I found interesting and those I chose to ignore. I may

Rich and poor in Hong Kong

not recall exactly every civil rights rally or Vietnam War protest I took part in, but I once was tear gassed when storming a Pentagon entrance. That's hard to forget. But then I wonder, did I really join with those who, at another time, attempted to levitate that building by projecting massive amounts of psychic energy onto it?

It took some digging but I recently recalled that after being angered by another Vietnam atrocity reported on the evening news, I went into the bathroom and burned my draft card in the sink. That was followed by public draft card burnings, when I must have burned my library card or something made to look like a draft card.

I recall being in trouble with the bishop in Hong Kong because of the way I sometimes celebrated Mass. Some of us were very creative with the liturgy in those days. When I look back at essays and articles I wrote during those years, I see both the strength and naïveté of youth. I know I didn't leave Maryknoll and my priesthood solely because of celibacy issues, but other than Maryknollers, it's mostly women I remember from my days in Ossining and Hong Kong.

I learned during my Maryknoll years the importance of rejoicing in the diversity of creation, in all its beauty, sacredness, and chaos. This learning began at the Venard where, as a 14-year-old Midwesterner, I lived with students from many other regions of the country, some even from other countries. The Specials were several years older than I and many were vets from the military. We were all very different, yet striving for the same goal: to serve as Maryknoll missioners.

My learning continued at Glen Ellyn where the early effects of Vatican II entered my life. The promise of Vatican II, along with the civil rights movement and my growing awareness of the Vietnam War, propelled me into taking advantage of the new openness at the Major Seminary. While there I experienced firsthand the beauty of multiple religious traditions, thereby deepening my respect for diversity in spiritual practice.

My Maryknoll education put me in a position to earn a decent salary during my years of employment. I do have a very nice home and that may simply be a reflection of my life in Maryknoll's many fine buildings, but I've never gotten into seeking possessions. During the 1970s when our children were young, Kathy and I lived on a small farm where we raised and preserved most of the food we consumed. At that time, Kathy chose to be mostly a stay-at-home mom to our four children, except when she was serving jail time for protesting Reagan era nuclear policies or was traveling to Central America on missions of friendship.

For many years after departing Maryknoll, I worked in the field of adoption and foster care. I take pride in my contributions to issues of transracial or transcultural adoption and to the empowerment of foster and adoptive parents. I firmly believe my effectiveness as a workshop leader, speaker, and writer on those subjects springs from the love of diversity and respect for the cultures and customs of others, something I learned at Maryknoll. I acknowledge my deep debt to Maryknoll and all those who contributed to the work of the Society and my education during the 15 years I was there.

Where have all the flowers gone? My generation flowered at Maryknoll and that flowering has continued throughout our lives. I can only speak for myself. I will always identify myself as a Catholic and a Maryknoller—I am too rooted in both to do otherwise —but the Roman Catholic Church and I have gone in different directions during recent years. Maybe it's just that I've lost interest in that Church. Or maybe I'm still learning about diversity, chaos, beauty, and sacredness in the world and have chosen to explore my personal path without a guide.

❑

Al Stumph ('68) lives in Chatham, N.Y., about 100 miles north of Maryknoll. After retiring from social services work in 2001, Al began doing lawn care for his neighbors, building wooden furniture for sale, and assisting his wife, Kathy Kinyon, in her antiques store. Kathy and Al have four children and seven grandchildren who are teaching them how to enjoy this latest stage of their lives.

Maryknoll to Africa:
By a Different Course

Thomas J. Hinnebusch ('66)

THE ENTIRE ORIENTATION OF MY LIFE—my career and my vocation as a married man and father—comes from Maryknoll, literally and figuratively. My story follows.

I graduated from St. Wendelin High School in Pittsburgh in June 1957. During my junior year I had made a decision to become a missioner, overwhelmed emotionally and spiritually by reading a biography of St. Francis Xavier and the story of his missionary zeal in India and the Far East. I talked with my Dominican uncle, Father John Hinnebusch, O.P., about joining the White Fathers, but he advised me against it and told me about Maryknoll. He also arranged through a confrere for me to be tutored in Latin by Sr. Marietta, a Sister of Charity. Advised that I would be studying Latin as a "special student," I wanted to get a head start.

Because construction was still going on at Glen Ellyn, the special students were sent to the Venard until after Christmas when we moved to Glen Ellyn. I was on my way, focused on being a priest and missionary. During my senior year, however, I was reassessing my vocation. After reading the writings of Thomas Merton, I found the life of a Trappist attractive and seductive. At the same time I was being pulled in another direction. While home during the summer of 1961, I spent time with my younger brother Paul and his wife, Peggy, who had married the summer before—I had, in fact, been their best man. Their son Matthew had been born that June. As I held that little baby boy in my arms, married life and children appealed to me.

By August I was at Bedford, where the few months I spent at the novitiate passed as in a dream. I tried being a good novice, but I was miserable and unhappy. Father Art Kiernan had been assigned as my spiritual advisor, but I was in no hurry to see him. Finally, when I told him I was no longer sure I had a vocation to the priesthood, he shocked me by saying that he knew. "I have been watching you," he said. Kiernan made it easy. He told me I had to make up my mind, either make a commitment to go on to ordination or leave and not look back.

Back in his office a week later, I told him I was leaving. "What now?" he responded. I told him that because of my Latin and Spanish, I had developed a strong interest in languages and thought I would go to Duquesne University to do a master's degree in a modern foreign language. Then in a single moment of time everything in my life changed! Kiernan told me about an African Studies and language program at Duquesne. He knew about it because two Maryknollers had been studying Swahili there before taking up their assignments in East Africa. Kiernan didn't know it then, but he set the course of my life's career. By February 1962 I was studying African Studies at Duquesne and that summer I started Swahili, little realizing how profoundly I was setting the stage for my future.

At Duquesne, I met my wife, Claudia Kessler, who was in her senior year studying biology with a minor in English. We married in August 1963, and in January 1964 I finished my M.A. with a lot of help from her. A job with the government had fallen through, and Claudia and I began talking about volunteer teaching opportunities in Africa. As an interim job, I replaced a Latin and English teacher in a suburban Pittsburgh middle school, where I discovered that I had the self-confidence to teach, and to teach well. Another turning point!

Late in the spring of 1964, Director of the African Institute Geza Grosschmid asked me to teach Swahili during the summer in a cooperative African Language Program supported by funding and with professors from other universities: Columbia, Indiana, Northwestern, and the University of California at Los Angeles. With some trepidation I accepted; after all, while I had studied the language for the equivalent of six semesters, my proficiency was only that of a beginner with no Africa experience. Even so, the summer went well. I learned a lot about language teaching methodology from the other teachers, especially Dr. Bill Welmers from UCLA where I eventually did my PhD. Then, another surprise: Grosschmid offered me a year-long job teaching elementary level Swahili at Duquesne. I jumped at the chance. During the interim, I taught a special Swahili course at the University of West Virginia to a group of vocational agriculture teachers on USAID contract to teach in East Africa. I commuted to Morgantown, returning to Pittsburgh on the weekends. It was lonely being away from home, especially since Claudia had just given birth to our first child, David, a week into the course. Another milestone!

During the year I taught at Duquesne, I did a year-long M.A. in linguistics in a new program at the University of Pittsburgh. In the meantime Claudia and I continued to talk about going to Africa to teach. In January 1965, after the meeting of the Modern Language Association in New York City, I went up to Ossining to visit my classmates who were still a year away from ordination. When I was talking with Ziggy Jamroz, I told him about our interest in doing volunteer work in Africa. He introduced me to Father Gerry Grondin, a member of the Council and former prefect apostolic of the Diocese of Musoma, Tanzania. After I told him my story, he asked if I was interested in working at the language school in Musoma. I left that day with a three-year commitment to work in Tanzania for Maryknoll. We never thought of it at the time, but we became the first Maryknoll lay missioners in East Africa, a decade before the Maryknoll Lay Missioner program was officially established.

Eight months later Claudia and I and our one-year-old son David were in Musoma. I worked under the supervision of Maryknoll Father Phil Sheerin and Maryknoll Sister Anita MacWilliams. Initially I was supposed to do an analysis of the local language, Kwaya, spoken then by about 30,000 people in the region. I started the work, but within a few months Maryknoll Bishop John J. Rudin of Musoma had decided that the national language, Swahili, would be used in all diocesan work. I began working with Anita on an elementary teaching manual of Swahili. This subsequently became the model for my widely used elementary Swahili text published in the late 1970s and still a best-seller today. My other duties included teaching Swahili grammar, African studies courses, and helping in the training and supervision of our local African teachers.

Claudia, in the meantime, began teaching biological sciences and English at the St. Pius X diocesan minor seminary. We were living in a prefabricated wooden "chalet" with a magnificent view of Lake Victoria. It was a perfect location, close to our respective places of work. Also close by were a girls' school founded and run by the Maryknoll Sisters and a convent of African nuns, the Immaculate Heart Sisters.

We were part of a community—or so we thought. The Second Vatican Council (1962–1965) was just beginning to influence the lives and vocations of the nuns and priests. The notion of lay persons as ministers of the Gospel was a new experience for everyone involved. We not only had to adapt to a new country and culture, but to a clerical community that wasn't sure how to work us into the mix. Though there were bumps in the road for all of us, Claudia and I look back on those three years with Maryknoll as some of the best in our 48 years of marriage.

Professionally, the time with Maryknoll at Glen Ellyn, Bedford, and Tanzania led me to an academic career of teaching and research. Without my time at Glen Ellyn and then Bedford, I am sure my life and career would be quite different today. I don't dwell on what might have been, and I truly have no regrets. While I did leave Maryknoll, in many ways I never did. The final line of Robert Frost's poem, "The Road Not Taken," always comes to mind when I think about my journey: "I took the one less traveled by, And that has made all the difference."

❏

After Musoma, Tom gained his PhD in linguistics from UCLA, where he now is Professor Emeritus of Linguistics and African Languages. He and his wife Claudia live in Los Angeles. They have three grown children, David, Cathy, and Andrew; and five grandchildren, Melissa, Shanna, Aiden, Penelope, and Thibaud.

Your Works Are Wonderful
(Just As They Are)

Bill Murphy ('71)

I KNEW I HAD TO MAKE A DECISION, but I was immobilized. I had been on a leave of absence for over a year, but I somehow couldn't get beyond the fear that I had made a promise to God and myself to be a priest, a missioner, and a celibate (a Maryknoller) and that if I broke that promise I would somehow rupture my relationship with God. That thought terrified me. I stood like a deer facing a set of headlights.

I had been in Maryknoll since I was a teenager, was ordained in 1971, worked in Tanzania, East Africa, for five years, and then in the States in the Society's Development and Communication Departments. But I knew something was wrong. I wasn't happy in my work or with myself. I was depressed and although my superiors at Maryknoll couldn't have been more patient and supportive, all the therapy, counseling, and pills weren't helping. If I broke my promise, would I ruin my relationship with God?

I received my answer while on a retreat. I read Psalm 139:

> *O Lord, you have searched me and you know me.*
> *You know when I sit and when I rise; you perceive my*
> *thoughts from afar.*
> *You discern my going out and my lying down;*
> *You are familiar with all my ways.*
> *Before a word is on my tongue you know it completely,*
> *O Lord.*
> *You hem me in—behind and before; you have laid*

183

Maryknoll Novitiate, Bedford, Massachusetts

your hand upon me.
Such knowledge is too wonderful for me, too lofty for
me to attain.
Where can I go from your Spirit? Where can I flee from
your presence?
If I go up to the heavens, you are there;
If I make my bed in the depths, you are there.
If I rise on the wings of the dawn, if I settle on the far
side of the sea, even there your hand will guide
me, your right hand holds me fast.
If I say, "Surely the darkness will hide me and the
light become night around me,"
even the darkness will not be dark to you;
the night will shine like the day,
for darkness is as light to you.
For you created my inmost being; you knit me
together in my mother's womb.
I praise you because I am fearfully and wonderfully
made;
Your works are wonderful, I know that full well....

184

I also read Matthew's telling of the Passion of Our Lord: the Lord's supper, Gethsemane, the betrayal by Judas, Peter disowning Jesus, Jesus before Pilate, the death and resurrection of Jesus, and finally the great commission: "And surely I am with you always, to the very end of the age."

The psalm and Matthew's account of Our Lord's Passion taken together convinced me that I am fearfully and wonderfully made (just the way I am—not as I would like me to be) and that the life, death, and resurrection of Jesus demonstrated that God made the covenant. There was nothing I could do that would break it. I did not actually leave Maryknoll and the priesthood for almost another year, but from that time forward, I felt I really had the option to listen to my mind, my body, and my soul, and to follow what I heard.

I am eternally grateful to the Society and the leadership, especially Fr. Jack Halbert, that they gave me time, space, and support, including financial, to find my way. I left Maryknoll and the priesthood and celibacy as sincerely as I had entered it. A year and a half later, in 1983, my wife, Jane, and I married, and I have never felt as happy or as holy.

❑

Bill Murphy was born in San Francisco in 1944 and entered the Maryknoll Junior Seminary at Los Altos in 1958. He was ordained in 1971 and went to Tanzania, East Africa. Bill married his wife, Jane Zampitella, in 1983 and both continue to thrive doing a variety of educational and community-building activities.

The Accidental Missionary

John O'Connor ('72)

I FIRST WENT TO OSSINING when I was about seven or eight. My best friend, Bobby Potterton, and I had accompanied his mother to visit her mother, Bobby's grandmother, at a Swedish Methodist nursing home in the town. It was a long trip in those days from Brooklyn and Bobby's mother was a serious visitor. And we weren't, so we used to go to the little stream behind the home and go exploring upriver for fish and frogs; and after a long time, we came to a cemetery and huge buildings. As we went exploring, we found a bunch of "priests" playing pool in their robes.… And they welcomed us in and even drove us back to town. *It was fun and I remembered.*

As the oldest son in an Irish Catholic family that hadn't had a priest in memory, I was going to be a priest even before I was born. After my birth, the first stop was the convent chapel and altar where the promise was sealed. I fought the ordination (and probably still do) as I led a religiously split life—sometimes very good and sometimes not so good. Got to be an altar boy—even after a not so good start—and attended Mass almost daily till after I left Maryknoll years later. I loved going to the first Mass and, if the altar boy didn't show up, I would jump from my pew and rescue the priest. *It was fun and I remembered.*

After getting through eight years of a Catholic grade school with a succession of Sister Mary's, I had to choose a high school —as if there was any choice. (I wanted to go to a public math school and the family thought the seminary was a better choice.) So on the same day that I "chose" the seminary, and after a half hour of stuffing a ballot box at a hardware store opening and winning a plastic set of bathroom accessories, my mother proclaimed without any hesitation that this win was clearly God showing that I had made the right decision.

I went to Cathedral High where I learned very little Latin, but was still good in math. However, the geometry priest believed that only God got 100s, so my perfect State Regents score was a 99.... Well, I can't complain as I had a lot more "mercy marks" than that perfect one. I enjoyed high school because I played handball well.... So well that the physics teacher put me in the lab group with the three smartest guys, so that even a zero on the final would have given me a pass. I enjoyed the handball. *It was fun and I remembered.*

But the diocesan seminary was way too traditional and boring... and it seemed to me that there were classmates already signing up to go to Rome or the largest Brooklyn parishes. I wanted "a little adventure." Like many others, I had cut my teeth on the stories of Isaac Jogues, Francis Xavier—now there was adventure. So to show the depth of my vocation I tried the Capuchin Franciscans because they were allowed to grow beards! Still, I did remember my encounter with the Knollers and so one day I took the subway to the recruiting center in Manhattan. I can't remember the priest's name, but I do remember his enthusiasm about mission and my possibility. He had signed me up for The Christophers ("Light one candle and you can change the world") program before I left...and it seems to me that Father Al Smith was at my home before I got there. My parents were impressed, as he had the same name as a Catholic presidential candidate. I liked Maryknoll's "weirdness" and enthusiasm and they weren't hung up in the past. *It was fun and I remembered.*

When I arrived at the front doors of Glen Ellyn, there was Tom Wilcox and he called me by name, and the same for everyone else who had just arrived. I will never forget that hospitality though I have never come close. What the most important part of GE was were the classmates. All of us seemed to be on the same page despite our varied geography or personalities. We were going to change the world. Vatican II tore into our inherited piety and worldviews. We were never to be the same again. At our Investiture the band played "A Mighty Fortress is our God." Truly, a sign about my future thought, they did change the "Papist foe" words.

It was fun and I remembered.

Hingham brought more changes—except that Tom stayed with us! We were to be the guinea pigs for a Clinical Pastoral Education Unit at Boston City Hospital. I had become a student at GE and now I was beginning to be a pastor. I learned that I really didn't know all that much about people. The remnant of the original 144 freshmen was down by a hundred...and more were to go. The liberal enthusiasm of Maryknoll and Vatican II got replaced with cautious liturgical sacramentalism. It was not fun.

I had the opportunity to "work" with an Episcopal ministry in East Los Angeles. It was a wonderful team ministry that exploited everyone's strengths. I also learned again that Tom was right when he told me after my first Latin exam that I would never be a Latin teacher. *It was fun and I remembered.*

Most of my close friends had left by the time I hit the Knoll. And I felt like I did when I was leaving Cathedral. During my short stay we took a clinical course at New York Theological. A Lutheran deaconess and I were together for the Moratorium. *It was fun again and I remembered.*

And I left Maryknoll...physically. I do think that my worldview from politics, missions, interfaith dialogue, and respect for the value of clinical education and dedication to vocation was cemented in my soul during my time there.

Since then I married that Lutheran deaconess and we emigrated to Canada in order to finish my education and prepare for ordination with the Lutheran Church of America. However, I am still in Canada 40 years later. Sister Joan and I had two children, Kristin ('72) and John Aaron ('74). I was ordained in 1973 and went to a small town church in Hespeler, Ontario, for six years. The Lutheran Church at the time was appealing, as the conviction of the individual conscience was highlighted. In some ways it was the institutionalization of an informal motto of my Maryknoll experience. *It was fun and I remembered.*

Parish life was not really for me—just a little too slow and predictable. During those parish years I went on to become a dreaded CPE supervisor and AAMFT supervisor. Then I was given an opportunity for the job of my life. I secured the chaplain's position at McMaster University Medical Centre in Hamilton. In many ways it was a secular Maryknoll...new, different, nonhierarchical. I got involved in almost everything—what an adventure! And, of course, physicians are definitely mission territory. I learned so much as professionals and patients struggled honestly with the "meaning of life" without the required mantras of the seriously religious. *It was fun and I remembered.*

It stayed fun until the continued mergers converted a hospital to a corporation, and that was way too much for this child of the sixties. And there was this nagging urge to do something more. I talked the hospital into giving me a leave and headed off to the University of Mexico at Mérida to be the expert in changing teaching styles to the McMaster model of problem-based learning. My colleague, a pediatric intensivist, assured me that half the faculty talked English—so no problems. However, after I got there I found no one spoke English and by the end of the third week my Spanish teacher would break into tears when I showed up. Tom was right about me not having any language skills—Latin or otherwise. I had a great holiday and my Spanish could at least get me and my van all over Mexico and not impounded by the *policía.* I was obviously never going to be teaching in Spanish. *It was fun and I remembered.*

My marriage with my Deaconess Joan was not the easiest for me or our children. She was increasingly ill in many ways, and she died in 1991 . It took some time to get myself together and back in form to take on the world. I was not eager to get married again but/and a woman whom I had known for many years turned into an "interesting" woman. We were married in 2001. Anne is a Unitarian minister, and she has three children, Susan, Sara, and Christine. I do not think that we worked very hard, so it was more luck than anything else that we have achieved a functioning blended family. *It is fun and I remembered.*

I think it is partly because I have a great marriage that I can continue with my own journey. What I learned in Mexico was that I was never learning another language. I still wanted to do something as a "human being missionary." Well, I ended up in Guyana, South America, after Anne had told me that they speak English there. I went on the net and found the only health care facility with a website was St. Joseph Mercy Hospital. I wrote the CEO, Sister Sheila, who immediately *traded me back to a Lutheran psychiatrist* who was a well-known visitor to Guyana. I had to write her

again to say I just wanted to come as a human being. And come I did in 2002 for the first time and this fall during the 100th Anniversary I will be there for the ninth three-month tour. (If you'd like to read more, my journals are on line at www.revjoc.blogspot.com.]
It is fun and I remembered.

So how do I credit Maryknoll for my secular, irreverent, non-Catholic, agnostic-ish Lutheran self? My answer is probably colored by the nostalgia of the 100th, and that I was oblivious to the abuses of the faculty toward some of my classmates in those days. I am not the same person who left Ossining as a faculty member called me an "apostate." And yet, I am the same person. I do not know how to tease out what I owe Maryknoll for my present. There are so many variables in the forty years since.

It may not be something specific, but more a flavor. My belief in myself and my abilities were nurtured by my time with Maryknoll …by faculty, classmates, experiences, and by its vision in those days. Though those days are more than half my life ago, they were the beginning of who I have become.

I end with an Emily Bronte poem:

> I've DREAMT in my life dreams
>   That have stayed with me ever after,
> And changed my ideas;
>   They have gone through and through me,
> Like wine through water,
>   And altered the colour of my mind.

❏

John is a retired Lutheran pastor living in Nova Scotia who still regularly works in Guyana.

Blessed Am I

Ev Charette ('72)

Blessed am I with
    The Maryknoll relationships and
The Overseas Training Program in
    Tanzania, East Africa.
These missionary relationships
    And cross-cultural experiences
Shaped the ministry I now enjoy:
    Grandparenting and hospital chaplaincy.
With a great-full heart,
    I thank each and every one of you
For the ways you have nurtured my Spirit.

❑

Everett Charette entered Maryknoll Seminary in 1963. A highlight of his journey with Maryknoll was his experience in Tanzania from 1971 to 1973. After leaving Maryknoll, he moved to Minnesota to pursue lay ministry. He met the love of his life, Jane. They married and had two children, Jon and Julie. His ministry then expanded to hospital chaplaincy in Kalamazoo, Mich. The family moved to Toledo, Ohio, where Jane returned to high school administration and Ev continues his hospital chaplaincy work to this day. The children have grown, married, and gifted the world with three grandchildren, the fourth due in May 2011. His hobbies are grandparenting, genealogy, photography, and a healthy lifestyle.

My Life and Maryknoll

Charlie Lockwood ('71)

I **BELIEVE I BECAME THE PERSON I AM TODAY** because of the love of my parents, the support and love of my spouse, Peggy, and the incredible worldview and training I received in Maryknoll.

I was born the sixth of nine children, seven of whom were boys: a busy household, to say the least. I never knew until after I entered the seminary at the age of 14, that my parents first met each other at a card party whose purpose was to raise money for a Maryknoll missioner in China. Even before I was aware, the mission spirit of Maryknoll had touched my family.

As I reflect, I see many of my qualities and aspirations directly influenced by the men of Maryknoll, individually and in community.

When I made the long and difficult decision at age 24 to leave the seminary, I felt supported and still accepted by my superiors. Because of their wisdom, I never felt a sense of guilt or shame that I had not continued to ordination. To the contrary, my superiors reminded me that I was still called to mission. As a result, after choosing education in the health and wellness discipline as my career, I was motivated to do the hard work of becoming an excellent teacher and have for over 40 years guided and influenced the lives of hundreds students from sixth to twelfth grade. Many students have told me that my teaching touched them deeply. Students often do not care as much about what you know, but know deeply how much you care.

My training in the Scripture classes of Fr. John McConnell, as well as my philosophy BA and theology MA, enabled me to serve as the head catechist and mentor to other catechists in our parish's very vibrant catechumenate (RCIA) process for over 20 years. My ability to connect Scripture with the everyday lives of hundreds of catechumens, which I learned first at Maryknoll, has helped them live more faith-filled lives.

In my 40 years of marriage to Peggy, we both practiced the loyalty, commitment, and day-to-day love through good times and difficult ones, essential for a strong marriage. These are the very same qualities that were visible to me in the lives of Maryknoll missioners. Our unconditional love for each other has been a light for many and enabled us to raise two wonderful children who have a vision of service in their lives.

At a young age, I was introduced to the discipline and schedule of good time management offered by Maryknoll seminary. The habits of daily manual labor, study, prayer, and recreation made a mark in how I productively use time, getting chores and organizational tasks done, but still finding regular time for sport, physical fitness, and recreation with friends and family.

Peggy and I have had the privilege of experiencing the inspiring work of Maryknoll by traveling to Caracas, Venezuela (Mario deJesus), to Santa Cruz, Bolivia (Dudley Conneely), and to Hong Kong, China (Bob Astorino and Bill Galvin). Their work and that of so many others is a testament to the quality of mission Maryknoll has spread throughout the world.

Most of all, it is my faith in God, the pausing in prayer during a busy day and the living of a Christ-centered life, that has come from the extraordinary men of Maryknoll. They guided me and left their indelible mark on my character and my life.

For this gift of Maryknoll, I am deeply grateful.

REMEMBERING MARYKNOLL
TO RAISE UP STERLING MEN FOR GOD,
MARYKNOLL, MY MARYKNOLL . . .

How many times did we sing, with robust voices, those precious words?
How does one explain a Mystery?
Where to begin...
As I look back, what touched me deeply:

- the miraculous gift of mission Fathers Walsh and Price did perceive;
- the reach beyond ourselves, God's will to achieve;
- the Paschal Mystery to proclaim and believe.

How does one explain a Mystery?

Where to search...

As I look within to search who I am:

- I realize how the men of Maryknoll still deeply touch my every day;
- I observe how gospel values form my decisions in most every way;
- I hope the Holy Spirit will continue to inspire us as we pray.

How does one explain a Mystery?

Where to dream...

As we seek to transform the future:

- let us celebrate and consecrate these next one hundred years;
- let us continue to spread God's Good News without fears;
- let us go forward boldly until the Lord Jesus appears.

Amen. Alleluia. Lord Jesus, come in glory!

❏

After leaving the seminary in 1968, Charlie began a career as a health and wellness teacher for grades 6 to 12. He married Peggy Shea in 1971; they will celebrate 40 years of marriage in July. They have two wonderful children, Deirdre, 34, and Christopher, 27. For over 25 years, they were ministry leaders, leading the RCIA process in their very active Catholic church. They lived in New York, first on Long Island and then upstate in Suffern. After Charlie's retirement from teaching in June 2006, they moved to Vero Beach, Fla., where they enjoy the warmer weather and many outdoor activities. They have traveled extensively in Europe, Africa, and South America, and most recently to China. They have always tried to visit Maryknollers in mission in their travels.

Adsum Domine

Biff Jenney ('68)

ON A DAY IN JUNE OF 1965, I had just returned to my room after attending rehearsal for receiving the first minor orders toward ordination. Father Fedders called out my name in Latin, and I replied "Adsum Domine." Back in my room, I sat down and decided that it was time to go. I felt that if I went through the next day's ceremony, and repeated the vow I had taken after novitiate, I would be past the point of no return.

Of course I had thought of this through the year, but I seemed to have joined Maryknoll without extended soul searching, and I was leaving the same way. I never heard a voice calling me to a "vocation," but more of helping hands, God's helping hands, steering me to the seminary.

It was here at Maryknoll that I met my greatest friends and felt that together we were all part of something. I learned that there is enough in this world. Enough food for all, if we share, enough love, if we give it to others, enough equity for those with no voice, if we help them speak. I learned that we can be examples of possibilities, if we reach out for all our brothers and sisters.

I may have told myself that it was the reading of Thomas Wolfe, and his books that chronicled the Gant family, or the great works of John Steinbeck, especially. The final scene of *The Grapes of Wrath*. During my final year, I attended a film seminar at Marymount College. The women in the course presented the feminine perspective; at that stage of my life I questioned celibacy and how it seemed to make it impossible to fully engage in the world. I told myself that these were the factors in my leaving, but forty years later, it seems more of "helping hands from the universe."

I was 20 when I joined Maryknoll and was about to turn 25 when I left. I had spent three full years living with my classmates on a 24/7 basis. I had grown up with them, prayed with them, and laughed with them. I loved them. I had friends on the faculty who helped me through times of self-discovery. I was friends with the Brothers, and I had friends in Ossining and the surrounding areas.

I didn't say goodbye to anyone. I left, on my own. I received one letter from Bruce Campbell, and Fr. Fedders did ask me to stay and reconsider. I can't believe that I just left, closing the door behind me. I considered that it was just the way it was. I was "called" but not chosen, I was the rich young man. I was leaving and could never again traverse that impenetrable barrier that suddenly came between me and the finest friends I will ever have, and we never said goodbye, good luck, stay in touch, nothing.

More collateral damage was the leaving of self behind. All the growth and self-discovery seemed to remain in the room I left. I emotionally took steps back to the way I was when I had graduated college three years earlier. Everything Maryknoll was placed on a shelf, and it gathered dust. I think my authentic self took a ten-year hiatus, beginning on that day in June with the words "Adsum Domine."

In 1968, when my classmates were being ordained, I was graduating law school. I called Maryknoll, to subscribe to the magazine, just to see the photographs of my friends in the ordination issue. They were beginning their journey, and I was beginning mine.

The practice of law began well. I was considered as good a young lawyer as any for the first few years. A feeling seemed to settle over me, a feeling that this was not the way I wanted my life to be. I was basically helping people develop real estate, and then producing tax shelters for them.

I don't know if there is any excuse or reason to become a drunk, no one made me drink, but drink I did. By 1975, the crash came, it always does, and I was both unemployed and unemployable. It came to a point where I had to make a threshold decision, an existential decision to live or die. My wife and son were in the picture, and I chose life. A start on living was to join Alcoholics Anonymous and get some help with the drinking.

It was at my first meeting, I listened to the speakers, and at the end we all stood up, joined hands and said the Our Father. Something happened. It wasn't the prayer, but an awareness that I was with a group, who saw or intuited that together we can find strength. There was hope, and the presence of possibilities of finding out who we were, and a realization that we had to be true to who we are, if we want to remain sober and avoid self destruction. I thought of Maryknoll, and the part of me that I had left there. I began to take it back.

A few months later, I was speaking at an AA meeting, and after the meeting a man came up to me, and asked me if I wanted a job in a court. The job would be temporary, and at an entry level, but there was room to grow and advance. The job was that of a probation officer, and the man offering it was one of the state deputy commissioners of probation.

I took the job, and decided to just be myself, my 25-year-old self. I was given an office, and I had a drawing of a circle within a circle placed on my door. The circle is a medieval sign that signified "beggars and gypsies are welcome here." Only a handful of people over the years knew the meaning of the circle, but I did, and it was a reminder to me not to forget what I discovered about myself at Maryknoll. Every time I see "Casablanca" I think of Bogart

Sunset on Concord River,
Maryknoll Novitiate, Bedford, Massachusetts

saying to Bergman,. "We'll always have Paris, we lost it for a while, but we got it back." I lost Paris for a while, but I got it back.

I began thinking that I had not left the priesthood or mission. The probate and family court became my region of mission, and my office became a parish. The sacraments became dignity and respect for the frightened, lonely, and desperate. I loved the job, and I am very grateful I found it.

The job went well, with promotions and appointments over the years, and in the late 1980s, out of the blue, my first issue of *Interchange* came, and I was in it. It was terrific to call and get calls from old friends. Maryknoll and the people associated with the Society are important to me. It is my hope that the alumni group calls out to others who have grown up in Maryknoll and give them the opportunity to come back to themselves.

❏

Biff Jenney lives in Wayland, Mass., with his wife Kate. They have one child, Bob, who is currently living in Houston. Biff retired from the Massachusetts Probate and Family Court in September 2009. Biff and Kate enjoy planning trips, trips they rarely take, but nonetheless plan, fully expecting to travel.

9279683R0

Made in the USA
Charleston, SC
28 August 2011